a gift of days

the greatest words to live by

stephen alcorn

Atheneum Books for Young Readers
New York London Toronto Sydney

An imprint of Simon & Schuster Children's Publishing Division

1230 Avenue of the Americas, New York, New York 10020

ATHENEUM BOOKS FOR YOUNG READERS is a registered trademark of Simon & Schuster,
Inc. For information about special discounts for bulk purchases, please contact
Simon & Schuster Special Sales at 1-866-506-1949 or business@simonandschuster.com.

The Simon & Schuster Speakers Bureau can bring authors to your live event. For
more information or to book an event, contact the Simon & Schuster Speakers Bureau at
1-866-248-3049 or visit our website at www.simonspeakers.com.

Book design by Debra Sfetsios

The text for this book is set in Minion Pro.

The portraits and patterns created for this book are polychrome relief–block prints; all have
been hand-painted by the artist on a variety of acid-free Mohawk papers.

Manufactured in China

First Edition

10 9 8 7 6 5 4 3 2 1

Library of Congress Cataloging-in-Publication Data

Alcorn, Stephen.

A gift of days: the greatest words to live by / Stephen Alcorn.—1st ed.

p. cm.

ISBN: 978-1-4169-6776-7

1. Alcorn, Stephen. 2. Celebrities—Portraits. 3. Celebrities—Quotations. I. Atheneum
Books for Young Readers. II. Title.

NE1300.6.A43A4 2008

769.92—dc22

2007048766

To the memory of
Fabrizio De André,
cantastorie extraordinaire

Illustrator's Note

IT WAS MY GOOD FORTUNE to come of age as an artist in the city of Florence, Italy, aka "the cradle of the Renaissance." Beyond every corner of this magical city lurks a poignant reminder of a glorious, bygone past, where the history of art is not only celebrated but venerated; a city in which streets, *piazze*, and schools bearing the names of Michelangelo, da Vinci, and Galileo abound, and in which monuments to cultural icons loom large and cast long shadows beneath the sun. It was under the spell *di Firenze* that I became an unabashed hero-worshiper—a penchant that found its first expression in a series of relief-block portraits of celebrated Italian artists begun in my teens, titled *Ritratti degli Artisti Più Celebri*. Whereas in my youth I often turned to the distant past for my subjects, now that I am older, paradoxically I find myself drawing ever-increasing inspiration from my contemporaries—the celebrated authors, painters, social activists, philosophers, and musicians of our age, several of whom (in particular those belonging to the last category) are young enough to be my brothers and sisters.

Amid the hustle and bustle of the streets of Porta Romana (a *quartiere popolare* located on the south side of the city, facing Rome) I attended the Istituto Statale d'arte di Firenze. There, my teachers stressed the importance of the humanities, encouraged the appreciation of genius, fostered an adherence to standards of excellence, and sought to impart genuine skills—a commitment I saw mirrored in the daily lives of the industrious artisans who gave the neighborhood so much of its charm and character. Then, across the Arno River, in the *quartiere* of San Marco, I saw for the first time an illustrated manuscript (in a fifteenth-century library of the Convento di San Marco; it is also where I first fell in love with the Book of Days genre). It is to these experiences that I trace the genesis of this book. Technically, the series of fifty-two portraits I've created embodies a larger, personal history, spanning more than thirty-five years, of experimentation in relief-block printmaking. It seems appropriate that the variety that exists within the pantheon of 366 cultural icons I've gathered be matched with my experimentation in ways to depict it.

It is my hope that above and beyond the 366 individuals celebrated herein, *A Gift of Days* will prove a fitting tribute to the life-affirming force of inspiration itself. Inspiration travels in mysterious ways and flows from a seemingly infinite variety of sources, and has a way of striking when one least expects. Often this takes place in the form of an epiphany. I recall with fondness the moments in which noble examples of such luminaries as Vincent van Gogh, Pablo Picasso, Albert Einstein, Martin Luther King Jr., Rosa Parks, Nina Simone, Bob Dylan, and Odetta Holmes (to name but a few) first entered into my life. Because of this recollection, I have come to associate inspiration with a moment of discovery. The thrill of revelation went hand in hand with an appreciation of the roles of individuals in our lives. With this appreciation came the inspiring realization that behind every beautiful song, article, poem, book, painting, speech— every righteous stance taken in the face of social injustice—there was a noble spirit at work, abiding by his or her conscience and engaging in a heroic effort to change and improve the world we live in. Distant echoes of the important cultural and political movements of my youth continue to resonate in my life. At the same time, new sources of inspiration continue to nourish and sustain me via the pages of newspapers, the walls of museums, the pages of books, the airwaves and the movements of the street. It is my belief that inspiration is everywhere to be found. It is up to us to recognize it. What better way to honor inspiration than to act upon it.

—S. A.

"I don't know whether I can, but I'll **try**."

—Betsy Ross

1   **Betsy Ross** (1752–1836), pacifist

2   **Isaac Asimov** (1920–1992), author

"The saddest aspect of life right now is that science gathers knowledge faster than society gathers wisdom."

3   **J. R. R. Tolkien** (1892–1973), author

"Not all who wander are lost."

4   **Sir Isaac Newton** (1643–1727), scientist

"To myself I am only a child playing on the beach, while vast oceans of truth lie undiscovered before me."

5   **Alvin Ailey Jr.** (1931–1989), dancer

"The creative process is not controlled by a switch you can simply turn on or off; it's with you all the time."

6   **Saint Joan of Arc** (ca. 1412–1431), political figure, martyr

"I am not afraid. . . . I was born to do this."

7   **Charles Samuel Addams** (1912–1988), artist

"I woke up the other night and felt like screaming. I thought, 'Why not? No one will ever hear me.' So I let out a long, thin scream, and felt much better."

8 Elvis Presley (1935–1977), entertainer

9 Simone de Beauvoir (1908–1986), author

"One's life has value so long as one attributes value to the life of others, by means of love, friendship, indignation, and compassion."

10 George Washington Carver (1864–1943), scientist

"When you do the common things of life in an uncommon way, you will command the attention of the world."

11 Alexander Hamilton (1757–1804), politician

"I think the first duty of society is justice."

12 Jack London (1876–1916), author

"The proper function of man is to live, not to exist. I shall not waste my days in trying to prolong them. I shall use my time."

13 Horatio Alger Jr. (1832–1899), author

"No period of my life has been one of such unmixed happiness as the four years [that] have been spent within college walls."

14 LL Cool J (1968–), entertainer

"I think when you move past your fear and you go after your dreams wholeheartedly, you become free. Know what I'm saying? Move past the fear."

wild

"They put me on television. And the whole thing broke loose. It was **wild**, I tell ya for sure."

—*Elvis Presley*

"**Nonviolence** is the answer to the crucial political and moral question of our time— the need for mankind to overcome oppression and violence without resorting to violence and oppression. . . . Man must evolve for all human conflict a method which rejects revenge, aggression, and retaliation. The foundation of such a method is love."

—*Martin Luther King Jr.*

15 **Martin Luther King Jr.** (1929–1968), civil-rights advocate

16 **Ethel Merman** (1908–1984), actress

"I preferred delivering my performance in person. I liked to be in control. You couldn't be in films."

17 **Benjamin Franklin** (1706–1790), inventor

"Hide not your talents. They for use were made. What's a sundial in the shade?"

18 **Oliver Hardy** (1892–1957), actor

"Here's another nice mess you've gotten me into."

19 **Edgar Allan Poe** (1809–1849), poet

"All that we see or seem/Is but a dream within a dream."

20 **Buzz Aldrin** (1930–), astronaut

"Mars is there, waiting to be reached."

21 **Christian Dior** (1905–1957), fashion designer

"Zest is the secret of all beauty. There is no beauty that is attractive without zest."

22 George Balanchine (1904–1983), choreographer

"First comes the sweat. Then comes the beauty—if you're *vairy* [sic] lucky and have said your prayers."

23 Édouard Manet (1832–1883), artist

"It is not enough to know your craft—you have to have feeling. Science is all very well, but for us, imagination is worth far more."

24 Edith Wharton (1862–1937), author

"Life is always a tightrope or a feather bed. Give me the tightrope."

25 Virginia Woolf (1882–1941), author

26 Angela Davis (1944–), professor, social activist

"We know the road to freedom has always been stalked by death."

27 Wolfgang Amadeus Mozart (1756–1791), composer

"Neither a lofty degree of intelligence nor imagination nor both together go to the making of genius. Love, love, love, that is the soul of genius."

28 Jackson Pollock (1912–1956), artist

"Today painters do not have to go to a subject matter outside of themselves. Most modern painters work from a different source. They work from within."

"That great Cathedral **space** which was childhood."

—*Virginia Woolf*

"I'd like to be remembered as a person who wanted to be **free** and wanted other people to also be free."

—*Rosa Parks*

29 Oprah Winfrey (1954–), entrepreneur

"I was raised to believe that excellence is the best deterrent to racism or sexism. And that's how I operate my life."

30 Franklin D. Roosevelt (1882–1945), former U.S. president

"Human kindness has never weakened the stamina or softened the fiber of a free people. A nation does not have to be cruel to be tough."

31 Jackie Robinson (1919–1972), athlete

"A life is not important, except in the impact it has on other lives."

february

1 Langston Hughes (1902–1967), poet

"Hold fast to dreams/For if dreams die/Life is a broken-winged bird/ That cannot fly."

2 James Joyce (1882–1941), author

"I am tomorrow, or some future day, what I establish today. I am today what I established yesterday or some previous day."

3 Gertrude Stein (1874–1946), author

"To write is to write is to write is to write is to write is to write is to write is to write."

4 Rosa Parks (1913–2005), civil-rights activist

5   **Hank Aaron** (1934–), athlete

> "My motto was always to keep swinging. Whether I was in a slump or feeling badly or having trouble off the field, the only thing to do was keep swinging."

6   **Babe Ruth** (1895–1948), athlete

> "Never let the fear of striking out get in your way."

7   **Laura Ingalls Wilder** (1867–1957), author

> "[I]t is the sweet, simple things of life which are the real ones after all."

8   **Kate Chopin** (1851–1904), author

9   **Alice Walker** (1944–), author

> "Helped are those who create anything at all, for they shall relive the thrill of their own conception, and realize a partnership in the creation of the Universe that keeps them responsible and cheerful."

10   **Mark Spitz** (1950–), athlete

> "I swam my brains out."

11   **Thomas Alva Edison** (1847–1931), inventor

> "I am proud of the fact that I never invented weapons to kill."

courageous

"And moreover, to succeed, the artist must possess the **courageous** soul . . . the brave soul. The soul that dares and defies."

—Kate Chopin

"All my life I have tried to pluck a thistle and plant a flower wherever the flower would **grow** in thought and mind."

—Abraham Lincoln

12 Abraham Lincoln (1809–1865), former U.S. president

13 Chuck Yeager (1923–), aviator/pilot

> "I was always afraid of dying. Always. It was my fear that made me learn everything I could about my airplane and my emergency equipment, and kept me flying respectful of my machine and always alert in the cockpit."

14 Frederick Douglass (ca. 1817–1895), abolitionist

> "No man can put a chain about the ankle of his fellow man without at last finding the other end fastened about his own neck."

15 Susan B. Anthony (1820–1906), suffragette

> "Principle, not policy; Justice, not favors. Men, their rights, and nothing more; Women, their rights and nothing less."

16 Heinrich Barth (1821–1865), explorer

> "After having traversed vast deserts of the most barren soil, and scenes of the most frightful desolation, I met with fertile lands irrigated by large navigable rivers and extensive central lakes, ornamented with the finest timber, and producing various species of grain, rice, sesamum, ground-nuts, in unlimited abundance, the sugar-cane, &c., together with cotton and indigo, the most valuable commodities of trade."

17 Michael Jordan (1963–), athlete

> "Talent wins games, but teamwork and intelligence wins [*sic*] championships."

18 Toni Morrison (1931–), author

> "I wrote my first novel because I wanted to read it."

19 Nicolaus Copernicus (1473–1543), astronomer

"The earth together with its surrounding waters must in fact have such a shape as its shadow reveals, for it eclipses the moon with the arc of a perfect circle."

20 Kurt Cobain (1967–1994), musician

"I'd rather be hated for who I am than loved for who I am not."

21 Nina Simone (1933–2003), singer

22 George Washington (1732–1799), former U.S. president

"It is far better to be alone than to be in bad company."

23 W. E. B. Du Bois (1868–1963), civil-rights activist

"[T]he cost of liberty is less than the price of repression. . . ."

24 Steven Jobs (1955–), businessman

"Innovation distinguishes between a leader and a follower."

25 George Harrison (1943–2001), musician

"As long as you hate, there will be people to hate."

"Yes, I'm a real **rebel** with a cause."

—Nina Simone

"You've got to know your **limitations**.
I don't know what your limitations are.
I found out what mine were when I was
twelve. I found out that there weren't too
many limitations, if I did it my way."

—*Johnny Cash*

26 Johnny Cash (1932–2003), musician

27 Ralph Nader (1934–), political activist

"The use of solar energy has not been opened up because the oil industry does not own the sun."

28 Linus Pauling (1901–1994), chemist

"Facts are the air of scientists. Without them you can never fly."

29 William H. Carney (1840–1908), soldier

"Boys, I only did my duty. The old flag never touched the ground."

march

1 Frédéric Chopin (1810–1849), composer

"Simplicity is the highest goal, achievable when you have overcome all difficulties."

2 Theodor Seuss Geisel (1904–1991) aka Dr. Seuss, author

"Be who you are and say what you feel, because those who mind don't matter and those who matter don't mind."

3 Alexander Graham Bell (1847–1922), inventor

"Concentrate all your thoughts upon the work at hand. The sun's rays do not burn until brought to a focus."

limitations

4 Miriam Makeba (1932–2008), singer

"Everyone now admits that apartheid was wrong, and all I did was tell the people who wanted to know where I come from how we lived in South Africa. I just told the world the truth. And if my truth then becomes political, I can't do anything about that."

5 Gerardus Mercator (1512–1594), cartographer

"I began to have doubts about the truth of philosophers."

6 Michelangelo (1475–1564), painter

7 Maurice Ravel (1875–1937), composer

"Music, I feel, must be emotional first and intellectual second."

8 Cyd Charisse (1921–2008), actress

"I wanted to be Gene Kelly. Well, really, I just wanted to dance with Cyd Charisse."

9 Ornette Coleman (1930–), musician

"You've got to realize. In the western world, regardless of what color you are, what title the music is, it's all played by the same notes."

10 Harriet Tubman (1820–1913), abolitionist

"I looked at my hands, to see if I was [the] same person now I was free. [There] was such a glory [over] e[v]erything, [t]he sun came up like gold [through] the trees, and [over the] fields, and I felt like I was in heaven."

"A **beautiful** thing never gives so much pain as does failing to hear and see it."

—*Michelangelo*

"Our battered suitcases were piled on the sidewalk again; we had longer ways to go. But no matter, the road is **life**."

—*Jack Kerouac*

11 Torquato Tasso (1544–1595), poet

"It is the fortunate who should extol fortune."

12 Jack Kerouac (1922–1969), author

13 Al Jaffee (1921–), artist

"To myself, without whose inspired and tireless efforts this book would not have been possible." *(in a book dedication)*

14 Albert Einstein (1879–1955), scientist

"Everything that can be counted does not necessarily count; everything that counts cannot necessarily be counted."

15 Sam "Lightnin'" Hopkins (1912–1982), musician

"People have learned how to strum a guitar, but they don't have the soul. They don't feel it from the heart. It hurts me. I'm killin' myself to tell them how it is."

16 James Madison (1751–1836), former U.S. president

"Liberty may be endangered by the abuses of liberty as well as by the abuses of power."

17 Mia Hamm (1972–), athlete

"I hope all you young girls see yourself up there. . . . We were just like you."

18 Queen Latifah (1970–), entertainer

19 Wyatt Earp (1848–1929), lawman, miner

"Fast is fine, but accuracy is everything."

20 Fred Rogers (1928–2003) aka Mr. Rogers, educator

"People often talk about play as if it were a relief from serious learning or a 'waste of time.' But for children, play *is* serious learning."

21 Johann Sebastian Bach (1685–1750), composer

"I worked hard. Anyone who works as hard as I did can achieve the same results."

22 Billy Collins (1941–), poet

"I think more people should be reading it [poetry] but maybe fewer people should be writing it. . . . There's an abundance of unreadable poetry out there."

23 Fannie Farmer (1857–1915), U.S. authority on cooking

"I certainly feel that the time is not far distant when a knowledge of the principles of diet will be an essential part of one's education. Then mankind will eat to live, be able to do better mental and physical work and disease will be less frequent."

24 William Morris (1834–1896), artist, author

"If you want a golden rule that will fit everything, this is it: Have nothing in your houses that you do not know to be useful or believe to be beautiful."

"I was taught from a young age that many people would treat me as a second-class citizen because I was African American and because I was **female**."

—*Queen Latifah*

"Love many things, for therein lies the true strength, and whosoever loves much performs much, and can accomplish much, and what is done in **love** is done well."

—*Vincent van Gogh*

25 Gloria Steinem (1934–), women's rights activist

"Without leaps of imagination, or dreams, we lose the excitement of possibilities. Dreaming, after all, is a form of planning."

26 Robert Frost (1874–1963), poet

"A poem begins in delight and ends in wisdom."

27 Ludwig Mies van der Rohe (1886–1969), architect

"Architecture is the will of an epoch translated into space."

28 Zbigniew Brzezinski (1928–), political scientist

"We cannot have that relationship if we only dictate or threaten and condemn those who disagree."

29 James E. Casey (1888–1983), businessman

"The basic principle [that] I believe has contributed more than any other to the building of our business . . . is the ownership of our company by the people employed in it."

30 Vincent van Gogh (1853–1890), artist

31 César Chávez (1927–1993), civil-rights activist

"There is no substitute for hard work, twenty-three or twenty-four hours a day. And there is no substitute for patience and acceptance."

1 Wangari Maathai (1940–), political activist

"The privilege of a higher education, especially outside Africa, broadened my original horizon and encouraged me to focus on the environment, women and development in order to improve the quality of life of people in my country in particular and in the African region in general."

2 Walter Percy Chrysler (1875–1940), businessman

"The real secret of success is enthusiasm."

3 Jane Goodall (1934–), anthropologist

"Change happens by listening and then starting a dialogue with the people who are doing something you don't believe is right."

4 Maya Angelou (1928–), poet

"History, despite its wrenching pain, cannot be unlived, but if faced with courage, need not be lived again."

5 Colin Powell (1937–), U.S. general

"If you are going to achieve excellence in big things, you develop the habit in little matters. Excellence is not an exception, it is a prevailing attitude."

6 Nadar (1820–1910), photographer

"The portrait I do best is of the person I know best."

7 Billie Holiday (1915–1959), musician

"No two people on earth are alike, and it's got to be that way in **music** or it isn't music."

—Billie Holiday

"Honesty is the first chapter in the book of **wisdom**."

—*Thomas Jefferson*

8 Betty Ford (1918–), former First Lady

> "Not my power, but the power of the position [as First Lady], a power which could be used to help."

9 Charles Baudelaire (1821–1867), author

> "A book is a garden, an orchard, a storehouse, a party, a company by the way, a counselor, a multitude of counselors."

10 Rachel Corrie (1979–2003), peace activist

> "We should be inspired by people . . . who show that human beings can be kind, brave, generous, beautiful, strong—even in the most difficult circumstances."

11 Joel Grey (1932–), actor

> "How satisfying it is to do theater that really has 'something important to say.'"

12 Herbie Hancock (1940–), musician

> "Music happens to be an art form that transcends language."

13 Thomas Jefferson (1743–1826), statesman, former U.S. president

14 Elizabeth Huckaby (1905–1999), educator

> "Things go on peacefully at school, if enforced peace is meant. The force isn't needed for most of the children . . . but for the few basically violent and the few more stirred to violence by emotionalism. . . . [T]he leaders in school and town [are] silenced by physical threats, principally to children, and by economic boycotts."

15 Leonardo da Vinci (1452–1519), artist

16 Wilbur Wright (1867–1912), inventor

"The desire to fly is an idea handed down to us by our ancestors who . . . looked enviously on the birds soaring freely through space . . . on the infinite highway of the air."

17 Nikita Khrushchev (1894–1971), politician

"The more bombers, the less room for doves of peace."

18 Clarence Darrow (1857–1938), attorney

"Chase after the truth like all hell and you'll free yourself, even though you never touch its coat tails."

19 Merce Cunningham (1919–), dancer

"My dance classes were open to anybody, my only stipulation was that they had to come to the class every day. . . ."

20 Joan Miró (1893–1983), artist

"The works must be conceived with fire in the soul but executed with clinical coolness."

21 Charlotte Brontë (1816–1855), author

"I am no bird; and no net ensnares me; I am a free human being with independent will."

"As a well-spent day brings happy sleep, so a life well spent brings **happy** death."

—*Leonardo da Vinci*

"How far that little candle throws his beams!
So shines a good **deed** in a naughty world."

—*William Shakespeare*

22 Immanuel Kant (1724–1804), philosopher

"Live your life as though your every act were to become a universal law."

23 William Shakespeare (1564–1616), poet, dramatist

24 Barbra Streisand (1942–), singer

"I've been called many names, like perfectionist, difficult, and obsessive. I think it takes obsession, takes searching for the details, for any artist to be good."

25 Edward R. Murrow (1908–1965), journalist

"Just once in a while, let us exalt the importance of ideas."

26 Eugène Delacroix (1798–1863), artist

"The artist who aims at perfection in everything achieves it in nothing."

27 Coretta Scott King (1927–2006), civil-rights activist

"Women, if the soul of the nation is to be saved, I believe that you must become its soul."

28 Harper Lee (1926–), author

"Before I can live with other folks I've got to live with myself. The one thing that doesn't abide by majority rule is a person's conscience."

29 **Duke Ellington** (1899–1974), composer

"A problem is a chance to do your best."

30 **Katherine Amelia Towle** (1898–1986), military officer, educator

"We worked very hard, but that's all part of the job, and of course I did enjoy it."

1 **Joseph Heller** (1923–1999), author

"There was only one catch and that was *Catch-22*. Orr would be crazy to fly more missions and sane if he didn't, but if he was sane, he had to fly them. If he flew them, he was crazy and didn't have to; but if he didn't want to, he was sane and had to."

2 **Benjamin Spock** (1903–1998), pediatrician

"All the time a person is a child, he is both a child and learning to be a parent. After he becomes a parent, he becomes predominantly a parent reliving childhood."

3 **Golda Meir** (1898–1978), politician

"A leader who doesn't hesitate before he sends his nation into battle is not fit to be a leader."

4 **Audrey Hepburn** (1929–1993), actress

"For beautiful eyes, look for the good in others; for beautiful lips, speak only words of kindness; and for poise, walk with the knowledge that you are never alone."

5 **Karl Marx** (1818–1883), philosopher

"Society does not consist of individuals, but expresses the sum of **interrelations**, the relations within which these individuals stand."

—*Karl Marx*

"The world is put back by the death of every one who has to sacrifice the development of his or her peculiar **gifts** to conventionality."

—Florence Nightingale

6 Sigmund Freud (1856–1939), psychologist

"The *interpretation* of dreams is the royal road to a *knowledge* of the unconscious *activities* of the mind."

7 Johannes Brahms (1833–1897), composer

"Without craftsmanship, inspiration is a mere reed shaken in the wind."

8 Harry S. Truman (1884–1972), former U.S. president

"America was not built on fear. America was built on courage, on imagination, and an unbeatable determination to do the job at hand."

9 Howard Carter (1874–1939), archaeologist

"All we have to do is to peel the shrines like an onion, and we will be with the king himself."

10 Bono (1960–), musician

"Music can change the world because it can change people."

11 Martha Graham (1894–1991), dancer

"Every dance is a kind of fever chart, a graph of the heart."

12 Florence Nightingale (1820–1910), nurse

13 Stevie Wonder (1950–), musician

"Just because a man lacks the use of his eyes doesn't mean he lacks vision."

14 Dante Alighieri (1265–1321), author

"Consider your origin; you were not born to live like brutes but to follow virtue and knowledge."

15 L. Frank Baum (1856–1919), author

"The road to the City of Emeralds is paved with yellow brick."

16 Louis "Studs" Terkel (1912–2008), author

"I've always felt, in all my books, that there's a deep decency in the American people and a native intelligence—providing they have the facts, providing they have the information."

17 Sugar Ray Leonard (1956–), athlete

"I want my fights to be seen as plays that have a beginning, a middle and an end."

18 Bertrand Russell (1872–1970), philosopher

"Do not fear to be eccentric in opinion, for every opinion now accepted was once eccentric."

19 Malcolm X (1925–1965), activist

"A man who **stands** for nothing will fall for anything."

—*Malcolm X*

"There is nothing so stable as **change**."

—*Bob Dylan*

20 Jimmy Stewart (1908–1997), actor

"Never treat your audience as customers, always as partners."

21 Andrei Dmitrievich Sakharov (1921–1989), physicist

"[B]oth now and for always, I intend to hold fast to my belief in the hidden strength of the human spirit."

22 Mary Cassatt (1844–1926), painter

"I think that if you shake the tree, you ought to be around when the fruit falls to pick it up."

23 Margaret Fuller (1810–1850), journalist

"If you have knowledge, let others light their candles in it."

24 Bob Dylan (1941–), musician

25 Ralph Waldo Emerson (1803–1882), poet

"Common sense is genius dressed in its working clothes."

26 Miles Davis (1926–1991), musician

"Don't play what's there, play what's not there."

27 Julia Ward Howe (1819–1910), author

"I shall stick to my resolution of writing always what I think no matter whom it offends."

28 Gladys Knight (1944–), musician

"We all have a responsibility, and since I've been so wonderfully blessed, I really want to share and to make life at least a little better. So every chance I get to share the gospel or uplift people, I will take full advantage of that opportunity."

29 John F. Kennedy (1917–1963), former U.S. president

"Conformity is the jailer of freedom and the enemy of growth."

30 Benny Goodman (1909–1986), musician

"[S]ometimes when you start losing detail, whether it's in music or in life, something as small as failing to be polite, you start to lose substance."

31 Walt Whitman (1819–1892), poet

june

1 Morgan Freeman (1937–), actor

"Black history is American history."

2 Thomas Hardy (1840–1928), poet

"Poetry is emotion put into measure. The emotion must come by nature, but the measure can be acquired by art."

"I believe a leaf of grass is no less than the **journey**-work of the stars . . ."

—Walt Whitman

"The writer's joy is the thought that can become emotion, the **emotion** that can wholly become a thought."

—Thomas Mann

3 Allen Ginsberg (1926–1997), poet

"Poetry is the one place where people can speak their original human mind. It is the outlet for people to say in public what is known in private."

4 Socrates (ca. 470 BC–399 BC), philosopher

"The greatest way to live with honor in this world is to be what we pretend to be."

5 Bill D. Moyers (1934–), journalist

"Whenever I learn something new—and it happens every day—I feel a little more at home in this universe, a little more comfortable in the nest."

6 Thomas Mann (1875–1955), author

7 Nikki Giovanni (1943–), poet

"If now isn't a good time for the truth, I don't see when we'll get to it."

8 Frank Lloyd Wright (1867–1959), architect

"Every great architect is—necessarily—a great poet. He must be a great original interpreter of his time, his day, his age."

9 Michael J. Fox (1961–), entertainer

"One's dignity may be assaulted, vandalized, and cruelly mocked, but cannot be taken away unless it is surrendered."

10 Judy Garland (1922–1969), entertainer

"I've always taken *The Wizard of Oz* very seriously, you know. I believe in the idea of the rainbow. And I've spent my entire life trying to get over it."

11 Jacques-Yves Cousteau (1910–1997), explorer

"The sea, once it casts its spell, holds one in its net of wonder forever."

12 Anne Frank (1929–1945), author

"It's really a wonder that I haven't dropped all my ideals, because they seem so absurd and impossible to carry out. Yet I keep them, because in spite of everything I still believe that people are really good at heart."

13 William Butler Yeats (1865–1939), poet

"But I, being poor, have only my dreams;/I have spread my dreams under your feet;/Tread softly because you tread on my dreams."

14 Harriet Beecher Stowe (1811–1896), abolitionist

15 Saul Steinberg (1914–1999), artist

"The artist is an educator of artists of the future . . . who are able to understand and in the process of understanding perform unexpected—the best—evolutions."

16 Tupac Shakur (1971–1996), entertainer

"I'm twenty-three years old. And I might just be my mother's child, but in all reality, I'm everybody's child. . . . Nobody raised me; I was raised in this society."

"The past, the present and the **future** are really one: [T]hey are today."

—Harriet Beecher Stowe

"It was a **time** when only the dead
smiled, happy in their peace."

—*Anna Gorenko aka Anna Akhmatova*

17 Igor Stravinsky (1882–1971), composer

"I know that the twelve notes in each octave and the varieties of rhythm offer me opportunities that all of human genius will never exhaust."

18 Sir Paul McCartney (1942–), musician

"I don't work at being ordinary."

19 Lou Gehrig (1903–1941), athlete

"There is no room in baseball for discrimination. It is our national pastime and a game for all."

20 Lillian Hellman (1905–1984), playwright

"I cannot and will not cut my conscience to fit this year's fashion."

21 Jean-Paul Sartre (1905–1980), philosopher

"A finite point has no meaning without an infinite reference point."

22 Erich Maria Remarque (1898–1970), author

"A hospital alone shows what war is."

23 Anna Gorenko (1889–1966) aka Anna Akhmatova, author

24 Robert Reich (1946–), politician

"A leader is someone who steps back from the entire system and tries to build a more collaborative, more innovative system that will work over the long term."

25 George Orwell (1903–1950), author

26 Derek Jeter (1974–), athlete

"You don't just accidentally show up in the World Series."

27 Helen Keller (1880–1968), author

"Everything has its wonders, even darkness and silence, and I learn, whatever state I may be in, therein to be content."

28 Mel Brooks (1926–), entertainer

"Every human being has hundreds of separate people living under his skin. The talent of a writer is his ability to give them their separate names, identities, personalities, and have them relate to other characters living with him."

29 Antoine de Saint-Exupéry (1900–1944), author

"A pile of rocks ceases to be a rock when somebody contemplates it with the idea of a cathedral in mind."

30 Robert D. Ballard (1942–), oceanographer

"It is a quiet and peaceful place—and a fitting place for the remains of this greatest of sea tragedies to rest."

"Big Brother is **watching** you."

—George Orwell

"Feet, what do I need you for when
I have wings to **fly**?"

—*Frida Kahlo*

1 **Lady Diana Spencer** (1961–1997), former princess of Wales, human-rights advocate

> "Carry out a random act of kindness, with no expectation of reward, safe in the knowledge that one day someone might do the same for you."

2 **Hermann Hesse** (1877–1962), poet

> "Happiness is a how; not a what. A talent, not an object."

3 **Franz Kafka** (1883–1924), author

> "A book should serve as the ax for the frozen sea within us."

4 **Nathaniel Hawthorne** (1804–1864), author

> "Happiness is a butterfly, which, when pursued, is always just beyond your grasp, but which, if you will sit down quietly, may alight upon you."

5 **Chuck Close** (1940–), artist

> "Painting is the most magical of mediums. The transcendence is truly amazing to me every time I . . . see how somebody figured another way to rub colored dirt on a flat surface and make space where there is no space or make you think of a life experience."

6 **Frida Kahlo** (1907–1954), artist

7 **Satchel Paige** (1905–1982), athlete

> "I never threw an illegal pitch. The trouble is, once in a while I toss one that ain't never been seen by this generation."

8 Elisabeth Kübler-Ross (1926–2004), psychiatrist

"Watching a peaceful death of a human being reminds us of a falling star; one of a million lights in a vast sky that flares up for a brief moment only to disappear into the endless night forever."

9 Tom Hanks (1956–), entertainer

"I love what I do for a living; it's the greatest job in the world[. B]ut you have to survive an awful lot of attention that you don't truly deserve, and you have to live up to your professional responsibilities. I'm always trying to balance that with what is really important."

10 Arthur Ashe (1943–1993), athlete

"My potential is more than can be expressed within the bounds of my race or ethnic identity."

11 E. B. White (1899–1985), author

"I would feel more optimistic about a bright future for man if he spent less time proving he can outwit Nature and more time tasting her sweetness and respecting her seniority."

12 Henry David Thoreau (1817–1862), author

13 Erno Rubik (1944–), inventor

"The problems of puzzles are very near the problems of life."

14 Woody Guthrie (1912–1967), musician

"Life has got a habit of not standing hitched. You got to ride it like you find it. You got to change with it. If a day goes by that don't change some of your old notions for new ones, that is just about like trying to milk a dead cow."

"As a single footstep will not make a **path** on the earth, so a single thought will not make a pathway in the mind. To make a deep physical path, we walk again and again. To make a deep mental path, we must think over and over the kind of thoughts we wish to dominate our lives."

—Henry David Thoreau

"**Somebody** must show that the Afro-American race is more sinned against than sinning, and it seems to have fallen upon me to do so."

—Ida B. Wells-Barnett

15 Thomas Bulfinch (1796–1867), author

"For mythology is the handmaid of literature; and literature is one of the best allies of virtue and promoters of happiness."

16 Ida B. Wells-Barnett (1862–1931), civil-rights advocate

17 Berenice Abbott (1898–1991), photographer

"Does not the very word 'creative' mean to build, to initiate, to give out, to act—rather than to be acted upon, to be subjective? Living photography is positive in its approach, it sings a song of life—not death."

18 Nelson Mandela (1918–), anti-apartheid activist

"I dream of the realization of unity of Africa whereby its leaders, . . . can write in their efforts to improve and to solve the problems of Africa."

19 Edgar Degas (1834–1917), artist

"It is all very well to copy what one sees, but it is far better to draw what one now only sees in one's memory. That is a transformation in which imagination collaborates with memory."

20 Sir Edmund Hillary (1919–2008), explorer

"It is not the mountain we conquer, but ourselves."

21 Ernest Hemingway (1899–1961), author

"Courage is grace under pressure."

22 Edward Hopper (1882–1967), artist

"Maybe I am not very human—what I wanted to do was to paint sunlight on the side of a house."

23 Raymond Chandler (1888–1959), author

"The more you reason, the less you create."

24 Amelia Earhart (1897–1939), aviator

25 Thomas Eakins (1844–1916), artist

"Enthusiasm for one's goal lessens the disagreeableness of working toward it."

26 Aldous Huxley (1894–1963), author

"Every man's memory is his private literature."

27 Norman Lear (1922–), director

"You can't change people's minds, but you can get them to think."

28 Jacqueline Kennedy Onassis (1929–1994), former First Lady

"One must not let oneself be overwhelmed by sadness."

"Never **interrupt** someone doing what you said couldn't be done."

—Amelia Earhart

"I am what time, circumstance, history, have made of me, certainly, but I am also much more than that. So are we all."

—James A. Baldwin

29 **Alexis de Tocqueville** (1805–1859), politician

"History is a gallery of pictures in which there are a few originals and many copies."

30 **Henry Ford** (1863–1947), entrepreneur

"Enthusiasm is the yeast that makes your hopes shine to the stars. Enthusiasm is the sparkle in your eyes, the swing in your gait. The grip of your hand, the irresistible surge of will and energy to execute your ideas."

31 **J. K. Rowling** (1965–), author

"The truth. It is a beautiful and terrible thing, and should therefore be treated with great caution."

august

1 **Yves Saint Laurent** (1936–2008), fashion designer

"Over the years I have learned that what is important in a dress is the woman who is wearing it."

2 **James A. Baldwin** (1924–1987), author

3 **Martha Stewart** (1941–), entrepreneur

"All the things I love are what my business is all about."

4 **Barack Obama** (1961–), U.S. president

"My parents shared not only an improbable love; they shared an abiding faith in the possibilities of this nation. They would give me an African name, Barack, or 'blessed,' believing that in a tolerant America your name is no barrier to success."

5 **Neil Armstrong** (1930–), astronaut

6 **Andy Warhol** (1928–1987), artist

> "Once you got Pop, you could never see a sign the same way again. And once you thought Pop, you could never see America the same way again."

7 **Garrison Keillor** (1942–), author

> "I think the most un-American thing you can say is, 'You can't say that.'"

8 **Emiliano Zapata** (1879–1919), revolutionary

> "I would rather die standing than live on my knees!"

9 **Marvin Minsky** (1927–), AI scientist

> "You don't understand anything until you learn it more than one way."

10 **Herbert Hoover** (1874–1964), former U.S. president

> "When there is a lack of honor in government, the morals of the whole people are poisoned."

11 **Alex Haley** (1921–1992), author

> "In every conceivable manner, the family is a link to our past, bridge to our future."

"Because I was born and raised in Ohio in a barn about sixty miles north of Dayton, and the legends of the Wrights have been in my memory for as long as I can remember."

—Neil Armstrong

"I'm tough, I'm **ambitious**, and I know exactly what I want."

—*Madonna*

12 Cecil B. DeMille (1881–1959), filmmaker

"What I have crossed out I didn't like. What I haven't crossed out I'm dissatisfied with."

13 Sir Alfred Hitchcock (1899–1980), director

"Self-plagiarism is style."

14 Steve Martin (1945–), entertainer

"I think I did pretty well, considering I started out with nothing but a bunch of blank paper."

15 Julia Child (1912–2004), chef

"Life itself is the proper binge."

16 Madonna (1958–), entertainer

17 Davy Crockett (1786–1836), frontiersman

"Be always sure you're right, then go ahead."

18 Robert Redford (1936–), entertainer

"Sundance [Film Festival] was started as a mechanism for the discovery of new voices and new talent."

ambitious

19 **William Jefferson Clinton** (1946–), former U.S. president

"There is nothing wrong with America that cannot be cured by what is right with America."

20 **Robert Plant** (1948–), musician

"I think that passion and love and pain are all bearable, and they go to make love beautiful."

21 **William "Count" Basie** (1904–1984), musician

"I'm saying: to be continued, until we meet again. Meanwhile, keep on listening and tapping your feet."

22 **Claude Debussy** (1862–1918), composer

"Music is the silence between the notes."

23 **Edgar Lee Masters** (1869–1950), poet

"To put meaning in one's life may end in madness,/But life without meaning is the torture/Of restlessness and vague desire—/it is a boat longing for the sea and yet afraid."

24 **Jorge Luis Borges** (1899–1986), author

25 **Althea Gibson** (1927–2003), athlete

"Shaking hands with the Queen of England was a long way from being forced to sit in the colored section of the bus going into downtown Wilmington, North Carolina."

dream

"Writing is nothing more than a guided **dream**."

—Jorge Luis Borges

"If we have no peace, it is because we have forgotten that we **belong** to each other."

—*Blessed Mother Teresa*

26 Blessed Mother Teresa (1910–1997), nun and social activist

27 Georg Wilhelm Friedrich Hegel (1770–1831), philosopher

"We do not need to be shoemakers to know if our shoes fit, and just as little have we any need to be professionals to acquire knowledge of matters of universal interest."

28 Rita Dove (1952–), author

"I carry a notebook with me everywhere. . . . But that's only the first step."

29 Charlie Parker (1920–1955), musician

"I realized by using the high notes of the chords as a melodic line, and by the right harmonic progression, I could play what I heard inside me. That's when I was born."

30 Robert Crumb (1943–), artist

"When people say 'What are underground comics?' I think the best way you can define them is just the absolute freedom involved . . . [W]e didn't have anyone standing over us."

31 Van Morrison (1945–), musician

"Music is spiritual. The music business is not."

september

1 Lily Tomlin (1939–), entertainer

"Life should be a little better, a little more honored and ennobled, rather than constantly debased."

2 **Christa McAuliffe** (1948–1986), educator

"I touch the future. I teach."

3 **Louis Sullivan** (1856–1924), architect

"Ornament and structure were integral; their subtle rhythm sustained a high emotional tension, yet produced a sense of serenity."

4 **Richard Wright** (1908–1960), author

"The impulse to dream had been slowly beaten out of me by experience. Now it surged up again and I hungered for books, new ways of looking and seeing."

5 **Louis XIV** (1638–1715), former king of France

"Every time I bestow a vacant office I make a hundred discontented persons and one ingrate."

6 **Jane Addams** (1860–1935), educator

"America's future will be determined by the home and the school. The child becomes largely what he is taught, hence we must watch what we teach him, and how we live before him."

7 **Grandma Moses** (1860–1961), artist

8 **Patsy Cline** (1932–1963), singer

"You're gonna have to learn to get out there in front of those cameras and hold your head up. Take charge when you're singing."

"I paint from the top down. From the sky, then the **mountains**, then the hills, then the houses, then the cattle, and then the people."

—*Grandma Moses*

"I always loved running—it was something you could do by yourself and under your own power. You could go in any direction, fast or slow as you wanted, fighting the wind if you felt like it, seeking out new sights just on the **strength** of your feet and the courage of your lungs."

—Jesse Owens

9 **Cesare Pavese** (1908–1950), poet

"One must look for one thing only, to find many."

10 **Roger Maris** (1934–1985), athlete

"You hit home runs not by chance but by preparation."

11 **O. Henry** (1862–1910), author

"Write what you like; there is no other rule."

12 **Jesse Owens** (1913–1980), athlete

13 **Roald Dahl** (1916–1990), author

"I began to realize that the large chocolate companies actually did possess inventing rooms, and they took their inventing very seriously."

14 **Allan Bloom** (1930–1992), philosopher

"Education is the movement from darkness to light."

15 **Dame Agatha Christie** (1890–1976), author

"Evil is not something superhuman, it's something less than human."

16 B. B. King (1925–), musician

"We all have idols. Play like anyone you care about but try to be yourself while you're doing so."

17 Hank Williams (1923–1953), musician

18 Lance Armstrong (1971–), athlete

"If children have the ability to ignore all odds and percentages, then maybe we can all learn from them. When you think about it, what other choice is there but to hope? We have two options, medically and emotionally: give up, or fight like hell."

19 Sir William Golding (1911–1993), author

"Novelists do not write as birds sing, by the push of nature. It is part of the job that there should be much routine and some daily stuff on the level of carpentry."

20 Sophia Loren (1934–), actress

"Beauty is how you feel inside, and it reflects in your eyes. It is not something physical."

21 Stephen King (1947–), author

"I am the literary equivalent of a Big Mac and fries."

22 Andrea Bocelli (1958–), singer

"Destiny has a lot to do with it, but so do you. You have to persevere, you have to insist."

"Hear that lonesome whippoorwill?/He sounds too blue to fly./The midnight train is whining low,/I'm so **lonesome** I could cry."

—Hank Williams

"I was born with music inside me. . . . Music was one of my parts. Like my ribs, my liver, my kidneys, my heart. Like my blood. It was a **force** already within me—like food or water."

—*Ray Charles*

23 Ray Charles (1930–2004), musician

24 Linda McCartney (1941–1998), photographer

"If slaughterhouses had glass walls, the whole world would be vegetarian."

25 William Faulkner (1897–1962), author

"Always dream and shoot higher than you know you can do. Don't bother just to be better than your contemporaries or predecessors. Try to be better than yourself."

26 Ivan Pavlov (1849–1936), physician

"Don't become a mere recorder of facts, but try to penetrate the mystery of their origin."

27 Samuel Adams (1722–1803), politician

"We cannot make events. Our business is wisely to improve them."

28 Ed Sullivan (1901–1974), television host

"If you do a good job for others, you heal yourself at the same time, because a dose of joy is a spiritual cure. It transcends all barriers."

29 Michelangelo Antonioni (1912–2007), director

"I can never understand how we have been able to follow these worn-out tracks, which have been laid down by panic in the face of nature."

30 Truman Capote (1924–1984), author

"I believe more in the scissors than I do in the pencil."

october

1 Jimmy Carter (1924–), former U.S. president

"America did not invent human rights. In a very real sense human rights invented America."

2 Mahatma Gandhi (1869–1948), political leader

3 Gore Vidal (1925–), author

"One is sorry one could not have taken both branches of the road. But we were not allotted multiple selves."

4 Buster Keaton (1895–1966), comedian

"My pictures are made without script or written directions of any kind."

5 Václav Havel (1936–), politician

"The salvation of this human world lies nowhere else than in the human heart, in the human power to reflect, in human modesty, and in human responsibility."

6 Fannie Lou Hamer (1917–1977), civil-rights activist

"'With the people, for the people, by the people.' I crack up when I hear it; I say, with the handful, for the handful, by the handful, 'cause that's what really happens. . . ."

"An eye for [an] eye only ends up making the whole **world** blind."

—*Mahatma Gandhi*

"All we are saying is give **peace** a chance."

—*John Lennon*

7 Desmond Tutu (1931–), activist

"If you are neutral in situations of injustice, you have chosen the side of the oppressor. If an elephant has its foot on the tail of a mouse and you say that you are neutral, the mouse will not appreciate your neutrality."

8 Jesse Jackson (1941–), civil-rights activist

"America is not a blanket woven from one thread, one color, one cloth."

9 John Lennon (1940–1980), musician

10 Thelonious Monk (1917–1982), musician

"All musicians are subconsciously mathematicians."

11 Eleanor Roosevelt (1884–1962), former First Lady

"Hate and force cannot be in just a part of the world without having an effect on the rest of it."

12 Luciano Pavarotti (1935–2007), musician

"If children are not introduced to music at an early age, I believe something fundamental is actually being taken from them."

13 Margaret Thatcher (1925–), politician

"It pays to know the enemy, not least because at some time you may have the opportunity to turn him into a friend."

14 **e. e. cummings** (1894–1962), poet

"The earth laughs in flowers."

15 **Isabella Bird** (1831–1904), author

16 **Oscar Wilde** (1854–1900), poet

"A dreamer is one who can only find his way by moonlight, and his punishment is that he sees the dawn before the rest of the world."

17 **Evel Knievel** (1938–2007), daredevil

"I guess I thought I was Elvis Presley, but I'll tell ya something. All Elvis did was stand on a stage and play a guitar. He never fell off on that pavement at no eighty miles per hour."

18 **Chuck Berry** (1926–), musician

"It's my love of poetry. A lyric is poetry with a melody— a message with a melody."

19 **John le Carré** (1931–), author

"I am still making order out of chaos by reinvention."

20 **Mickey Mantle** (1931–1995), athlete

"After I hit a home run I had a habit of running the bases with my head down. I figured the pitcher already felt bad enough without me showing him up rounding the bases."

"After I had ridden about ten miles the road went up a steep hill in the forest, turned abruptly, and through the blue gloom of the great pines which rose from the ravine in which the river was then hid, came glimpses of two mountains, about eleven thousand feet in height, whose bald gray summits were crowned with pure snow. It was one of those glorious surprises in scenery which make one feel as if one must bow down and **worship**."

—Isabella Bird

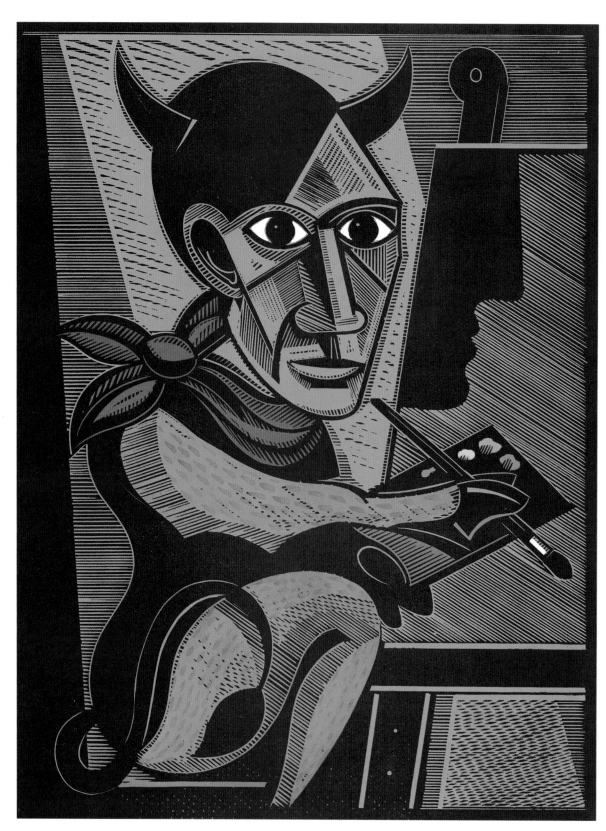

"Are we to **paint** what's on the face, what's inside the face, or what's behind it?"

—*Pablo Picasso*

21 **Alfred Nobel** (1833–1896), chemist

"It is my express wish that in awarding the prizes no consideration whatever shall be given to the nationality of the candidates, but that the most worthy shall receive the prize, whether he be a Scandinavian or not."

22 **Doris Lessing** (1919–), author

"Any human anywhere will blossom in a hundred unexpected talents and capacities simply by being given the opportunity to do so."

23 **Pelé** (1940–), athlete

"Enthusiasm is everything. It must be taut and vibrating like a guitar string."

24 **Paula Gunn Allen** (1939–), author

"For the American Indian, the ability of all creatures to share in the process of ongoing creation makes all things sacred."

25 **Pablo Picasso** (1881–1973), artist

26 **Hillary Rodham Clinton** (1947–), politician, former First Lady

"The challenge now is to practice politics as the art of making what appears to be impossible, possible."

27 **Dylan Thomas** (1914–1953), poet

"He who seeks rest finds boredom. He who seeks work finds rest."

28 Jonas Edward Salk (1914–1995), physician

"It is always with excitement that I wake up in the morning wondering what my intuition will toss up to me, like gifts from the sea. I work with it and rely upon it. It's my partner."

29 James Boswell (1740–1795), author

"A page of my journal is like a cake of portable soup. A little may be diffused into a considerable portion."

30 Ezra Pound (1885–1972), poet

"Genius . . . is the capacity to see ten things where the ordinary man sees one . . ."

31 John Keats (1795–1821), poet

"What the imagination seizes as beauty must be truth."

november

1 Stephen Crane (1871–1900), author

"You cannot choose your battlefield, God does that for you; But you can plant a standard where a standard never flew."

2 Marie-Antoinette (1755–1793), queen consort

"Courage! I have shown it for years; think I shall lose it at the moment when my sufferings are to end?"

3 Benvenuto Cellini (1500–1571), artist

"All men of whatsoever quality they be, who have done anything of excellence, or which may properly resemble **excellence**, ought, if they are persons of truth and honesty, to describe their life with their own hand."

—*Benvenuto Cellini*

"In seeking **truth** you have to get both sides of a story."

—*Walter Cronkite*

4 **Walter Cronkite** (1916–), newscaster

5 **Sam Shepard** (1943–), actor

> "Democracy's a very fragile thing. You have to take care of democracy. As soon as you stop being responsible to it and allow it to turn into scare tactics, it's no longer democracy, is it? It's something else. It may be an inch away from totalitarianism."

6 **John Philip Sousa** (1854–1932), composer

> "My religion lies in my composition."

7 **Albert Camus** (1913–1960), author

> "In the depths of winter I finally learned that there within me lay an invincible summer."

8 **Edmond Halley** (1656–1742), astronomer

> "This sight . . . is by far the noblest astronomy affords. . . ."

9 **Anne Sexton** (1928–1974), poet

> "Put your ear down close to your soul and listen hard."

10 **Martin Luther** (1483–1546), theologian

> "Even if I knew that tomorrow the world would go to pieces, I would still plant my apple tree."

11 Kurt Vonnegut Jr. (1922–2007), author

"We are what we pretend to be, so we must be careful what we pretend to be."

12 Grace Kelly (1929–1982), actress, former princess of Monaco

"The freedom of the press works in such a way that there is not much freedom from it."

13 Robert Louis Stevenson (1850–1894), author

"I never weary of great churches. It is my favorite kind of mountain scenery. Mankind was never so happily inspired as when it made a cathedral."

14 Claude Monet (1840–1926), artist

"I am following Nature without being able to grasp her, I perhaps owe having become a painter to flowers."

15 Georgia O'Keeffe (1887–1986), artist

16 W. C. Handy (1873–1958), composer

"Life is something like this trumpet. If you don't put anything in it, you don't get anything out."

17 Martin Scorsese (1942–), filmmaker

"Now more than ever we need to talk to each other, to listen to each other and understand how we see the world, and cinema is the best medium for doing this."

"I decided to start anew, to strip away
what I had been **taught**."

—Georgia O'Keeffe

"I have tried to depict what is true and not **ideal**."

—Henri de Toulouse-Lautrec

18 George Horace Gallup (1901–1984), statistician

"Polling is merely an instrument for gauging public opinion. When a president or any other leader pays attention to poll results, he is, in effect, paying attention to the views of the people. Any other interpretation is nonsense."

19 Ted Turner (1938–), entrepreneur

"The media is too concentrated, too few people own too much. There's really five companies that control 90 percent of what we read, see, and hear. It's not healthy."

20 Robert F. Kennedy (1925–1968), politician

"Ultimately, America's answer to the intolerant man is diversity, the very diversity which our heritage of religious freedom has inspired."

21 René Magritte (1898–1967), artist

"If the dream is a translation of waking life, waking life is also a translation of the dream."

22 Billie Jean King (1943–), athlete

"Be bold. If you're going to make an error, make a doozy, and don't be afraid to hit the ball."

23 Boris Karloff (1887–1969), actor

"The monster [Frankenstein] was the best friend I ever had."

24 Henri de Toulouse-Lautrec (1864–1901), artist

25 Joe DiMaggio (1914–1999), athlete

> "There is always some kid who may be seeing me for the first or last time. I owe him my best."

26 Sojourner Truth (ca. 1797–1883), abolitionist

> "I am not going to die, I'm going home like a shooting star."

27 Jimi Hendrix (1942–1970), musician

> "Knowledge speaks, but wisdom listens."

28 William Blake (1757–1827), poet

29 Louisa May Alcott (1832–1888), author

> "Let my name stand among those who are willing to bear ridicule and reproach for the truth's sake, and so earn some right to rejoice when the victory is won."

30 Sir Winston Churchill (1874–1965), politician

> "History will be kind to me, for I intend to write it."

december

1 Woody Allen (1935–), director

> "Life doesn't imitate art, it imitates bad television."

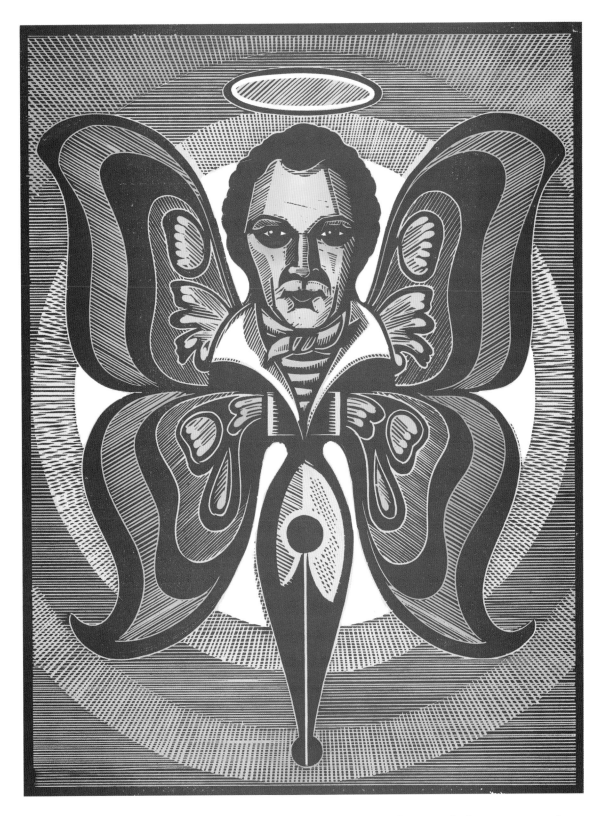

"I must create a system or be enslaved by another man's; I will not reason and compare: my business is to **create**."

—*William Blake*

2 **Maria Callas** (1923–1977), singer

"An opera begins long before the curtain goes up and ends long after it has come down. It starts in my imagination, it becomes my life, and it stays part of my life long after I've left the opera house."

3 **Jean–Luc Godard** (1930–), filmmaker

"To me style is just the outside of content, and content the inside of style, like the outside and the inside of the human body. Both go together, they can't be separated."

4 **Rainer Maria Rilke** (1875–1926), poet

"If your daily life seems poor, do not blame it; blame yourself; tell yourself that you are not poet enough to call forth its riches; because for the creator there is no poverty and no poor, indifferent place."

5 **Walt Disney** (1901–1966), producer and entrepreneur

6 **Ira Gershwin** (1896–1983), composer

"A song without music is a lot like H_2 without the O."

7 **Willa Cather** (1873–1947), author

"Desire is creation, is the magical element in that process. If there were an instrument by which to measure desire, one could foretell achievement."

8 **James Thurber** (1894–1961), author

"Humor is a serious thing. I like to think of it as one of our greatest earliest natural resources, which must be preserved at all cost."

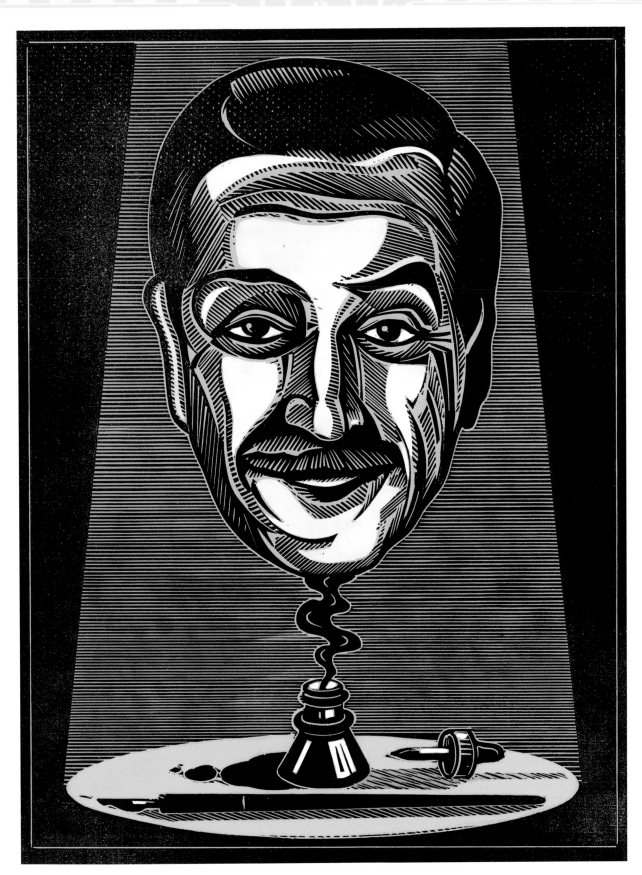

"A man should never neglect his **family** for business."

—*Walt Disney*

"**Forever** is composed of nows."

—Emily Dickinson

9 **John Milton** (1608–1674), poet

"I enjoyed an interval of uninterrupted leisure, which I entirely devoted to the perusal of the Greek and Latin classics."

10 **Emily Dickinson** (1830–1886), poet

11 **John Kerry** (1943–), politician

"I saw courage both in the Vietnam War and in the struggle to stop it. I learned that patriotism includes protest, not just military service."

12 **William Lloyd Garrison** (1805–1879), abolitionist

"Enslave the liberty of but one human being and the liberties of the world are put in peril."

13 **Dick Van Dyke** (1925–), entertainer

"I think it's being thrown at the wolves, we call it in our business."

14 **Shirley Jackson** (1919–1965), author

"I delight in what I fear."

15 **Julie Taymor** (1952–), director

"I use cinematic things in a theatrical way onstage, and in film I use theatrical techniques in a cinematic way."

forever

16 Margaret Mead (1901–1978), anthropologist

"Always remember that you are absolutely unique. Just like everyone else."

17 Ludwig van Beethoven (1770–1827), composer

18 Steven Spielberg (1946–), filmmaker

"I wanted to do another movie that could make us laugh and cry and feel good about the world. . . . This is a time when we need to smile more and Hollywood movies are supposed to do that for people in difficult times."

19 Édith Piaf (1915–1963), singer

"For me, singing is a way of escaping. It's another world. I'm no longer on earth."

20 Jean Racine (1639–1699), dramatist

"Nothing is so difficult but that it may be found out by seeking."

21 Frank Zappa (1940–1993), musician

"Most rock journalism is people who can't write, interviewing people who can't talk, for people who can't read."

22 Giacomo Puccini (1858–1924), composer

"Inspiration is an awakening, a quickening of all man's faculties, and it is manifested in all high artistic achievements."

"Music is the one incorporeal entrance into the higher world of **knowledge** [that] comprehends mankind but which mankind cannot comprehend."

—Ludwig van Beethoven

"No one can dub you with **dignity**. That's yours to claim."

—Odetta Holmes

23 Sarah Breedlove Walker (1867–1919) aka Madame C. J. Walker, philanthropist

"I have built my own factory on my own ground."

24 Joseph Cornell (1903–1972), artist

"Shadow boxes become poetic theaters or settings wherein are metamorphosed the element of a childhood pastime."

25 Clara Barton (1821–1912), humanitarian

"I may be compelled to face danger, but never fear it, and while our soldiers can stand and fight, I can stand and feed and nurse them."

26 Henry Miller (1891–1980), author

"Chaos is the score upon which reality is written."

27 Marlene Dietrich (1901–1992), actress

"It is a joy to find thoughts one might have, beautifully expressed with much authority by someone recognized wiser than oneself."

28 Woodrow Wilson (1856–1924), former U.S. president

"If a dog will not come to you after having looked you in the face, you should go home and examine your conscience."

29 Mary Tyler Moore (1936–), actress

"I'm not an actress who can create a character. I play me."

30 Tiger Woods (1975–), athlete

"It's the child's desire to play that matters, not the parent's desire to have the child play. Fun. Keep it fun."

31 Odetta Holmes (1930–2008), singer

January

Betsy Ross (Jan. 1, 1752–Jan. 30, 1836) American seamstress, a Fighting Quaker, and creator of the first American flag.

Isaac Asimov (Jan. 2, 1920–Apr. 6, 1992) Russian-born American author, best known for his science-fiction books.

J. R. R. Tolkien (Jan. 3, 1892–Sept. 2, 1973) British philologist and writer who authored *The Hobbit* and *The Lord of the Rings*.

Sir Isaac Newton (Jan. 4, 1643–Mar. 31, 1727) British physicist, mathematician, astronomer, natural philosopher, and alchemist.

Alvin Ailey Jr. (Jan. 5, 1931–Dec. 1, 1989) African-American modern dancer, choreographer, and founder of the Alvin Ailey American Dance Theater.

Saint Joan of Arc (Jan. 6, 1412–May 30, 1431) Fifteenth-century national heroine of France who was executed for heresy.

Charles Samuel Addams (Jan. 7, 1912–Sept. 29, 1988) American cartoonist, creator of *The Addams Family*, and brilliant practitioner of macabre humor.

Elvis Presley (Jan. 8, 1935–Aug. 16, 1977) American musician, actor, and cultural icon of mythic proportions.

Simone de Beauvoir (Jan. 9, 1908–Apr. 14, 1986) French metaphysical author, philosopher, and precursor of feminism.

George Washington Carver (ca. Jan. 10, 1864–Jan. 15, 1943) African-American scientist and botanist who was born into slavery and who revolutionized agriculture in the southern United States.

Alexander Hamilton (Jan. 11, 1757–Jul. 12, 1804) Founding Father and one of America's first constitutional lawyers.

Jack London (Jan. 12, 1876–Nov. 22, 1916) American author who wrote *The Call of the Wild*.

Horatio Alger Jr. (Jan. 13, 1832–Jul. 18, 1899) Nineteenth-century American author of dime novels who was best known for his rags-to-riches stories.

LL Cool J (Jan. 14, 1968–) Influential American hip-hop artist and actor.

Martin Luther King Jr. (Jan 15, 1929–Apr. 4, 1968) Martyred leader of the American civil-rights movement and recipient of the Nobel Peace Prize.

Ethel Merman (Jan. 16, 1908–Feb. 15, 1984) Tony and Grammy Award–winning American star of stage and film musicals.

Benjamin Franklin (Jan. 17, 1706–Apr. 17, 1790) Inventor, publisher, politician, coauthor of the Declaration of Independence, and one of the Founding Fathers of the United States.

Oliver Hardy (Jan. 18, 1892–Aug. 7, 1957) American comedian known for his role in one of the most celebrated comedy duos, Laurel and Hardy.

Edgar Allan Poe (Jan. 19, 1809–Oct. 7, 1849) American poet, short-story writer, literary critic, exponent of the American Romantic movement, and master of the detective-fiction genre.

Buzz Aldrin (Jan. 20, 1930–) American pilot, astronaut, and the second man to have set foot on the moon.

Christian Dior (Jan. 21, 1905-Oct. 23, 1957) French fashion designer and founder of Dior, a famous fashion house.

George Balanchine (Jan. 22, 1904–Apr. 30, 1983) Russian ballet choreographer whose work bridged the classical and modern forms of American ballet.

Édouard Manet (Jan. 23, 1832–Apr. 30, 1883) French painter of modern-life subjects and a pivotal figure in the birth of Impressionism.

Edith Wharton (Jan. 24, 1862–Aug. 11, 1937) American novelist who was the first female author to receive the Pulitzer Prize for literature.

Virginia Woolf (Jan. 25, 1882–Mar. 28, 1941) British novelist, essayist, and cofounder of Hogarth Press.

Angela Davis (Jan. 26, 1944–) American intellectual, social activist, and crusader for racial and gender equality.

Wolfgang Amadeus Mozart (Jan. 27, 1756–Dec. 5, 1791) Universally beloved musician and one of the most influential composers of the Classical era.

Jackson Pollock (Jan. 28, 1912–Aug. 11, 1956) Influential American painter and chief supporter of the abstract Expressionist movement.

Oprah Winfrey (Jan. 29, 1954–) American multiple Emmy Award–winning host of the *Oprah Winfrey Show*, the highest-rated talk show in television history.

Franklin D. Roosevelt (Jan. 30, 1882–Apr. 12, 1945) Thirty-second president of the United States. He was elected four times and was the only president to have served more than two terms.

Jackie Robinson (Jan. 31, 1919–Oct. 24, 1972) First African-American Major League Baseball player of the modern era, and forerunner of the Civil Rights Movement.

February

Langston Hughes (Feb. 1, 1902–May 22, 1967) African-American poet, novelist, playwright, and exponent of the Harlem Renaissance.

James Joyce (Feb. 2, 1882–Jan. 13, 1941) Innovative Irish expatriate who was best known for his novel *Ulysses* and the development of the stream-of-consciousness method.

Gertrude Stein (Feb. 3, 1874–Jul. 27, 1946) American expatriate writer, poet, feminist, and champion of Modern art, best known for her dictum "The rose is a rose is a rose is a rose."

Rosa Parks (Feb. 4, 1913–Oct. 24, 2005) African-American civil-rights activist whose refusal to give up her seat on a bus to a white person sparked the historic Montgomery Bus Boycott.

Hank Aaron (Feb. 5, 1934–) Legendary American baseball player, best known for having set the record for most career home runs (755), a record he held for thirty-three years.

Babe Ruth (Feb. 6, 1895–Aug. 16, 1948) Beloved American Major League Baseball player and larger-than-life celebrity.

Laura Ingalls Wilder (Feb. 7, 1867–Feb. 10, 1957) American author who is best known for the autobiographical and pioneer-based Little House series of children's books.

Kate Chopin (Feb. 8, 1851–Aug. 22, 1904) Protofeminist American novelist and short-story writer. Her tales had mostly a Louisiana Creole background. One of her best-known works is *The Awakening*.

Alice Walker (Feb. 9, 1944–) American author and feminist who is best known for her novel *The Color Purple*, for which she received the Pulitzer Prize.

Mark Spitz (Feb. 10, 1950–) American swimmer who had held the record for most gold Olympic medals won in the 1972 Olympic Games, and was the World Swimmer of the Year three times.

Thomas Alva Edison (Feb. 11, 1847–Oct. 18, 1931) Prolific American inventor who invented the incandescent lightbulb, and was one of the first people to employ the methods of mass production.

Abraham Lincoln (Feb. 12, 1809–Apr. 15, 1865) Sixteenth president of the United States and author of the Emancipation Proclamation and the Gettysburg Address.

Chuck Yeager (Feb. 13, 1923–) Retired brigadier general in the United States Air Force and the test pilot who became the man to travel faster than the speed of sound.

Frederick Douglass (ca. Feb. 14, 1817–Feb. 20, 1895) Eminent African-American abolitionist, author, and social reformer who was a participant of the Seneca Convention.

Susan B. Anthony (Feb. 15, 1820–Mar. 13, 1906) American civil-rights leader who started women's suffrage in the United States.

Heinrich Barth (Feb. 16, 1821–Nov. 25, 1865) German explorer and pioneer scholar of African culture.

Michael Jordan (Feb. 17, 1963–) Retired NBA superstar widely thought to be the greatest basketball player of all time.

Toni Morrison (Feb. 18, 1931–) African-American author, editor, professor, and author of the novel *Beloved*, for which she received the Pulitzer Prize.

Nicolaus Copernicus (Feb. 19, 1473–May 24, 1543) First astronomer to formulate a scientifically based heliocentric cosmology that displaced Earth from the center of the universe.

Kurt Cobain (Feb. 20, 1967–Apr. 5, 1994) Lead singer, guitarist, and cofounder of the influential Seattle-based rock group Nirvana.

Nina Simone (Feb. 21, 1933–Apr. 21, 2003) American singer, composer, and pianist who was active in the civil-rights movement.

George Washington (Feb. 22, 1732–Dec. 14, 1799) One of the Founding Fathers of the United States of America and the nation's first president.

W. E. B. Du Bois (Feb. 23, 1868–Aug. 27, 1963) African-American civil-rights activist, Pan-Africanist, sociologist, educator, historian, writer, editor, poet, and scholar.

Steven Jobs (Feb. 24, 1955–) American cofounder and CEO of Apple Computers, Inc.

George Harrison (Feb. 25, 1943–Nov. 29, 2001) British rock musician and lead guitarist of the Beatles.

Johnny Cash (Feb. 26, 1932–Sept. 12, 2003) Grammy Award–winning American country singer-songwriter and guitarist.

Ralph Nader (Feb. 27, 1934–) American political and consumer activist who ran for president of the United States in the 2000, 2004, and 2008 elections.

Linus Pauling (Feb. 28, 1901– Aug. 19, 1994) American quantum chemist and biochemist, two-time Nobel Prize Laureate, and peace activist.

William H. Carney (Feb. 29, 1840–Dec. 8, 1908) American Civil War hero and the first African American to be awarded the Congressional Medal of Honor.

March

Frédéric Chopin (Mar. 1, 1810–Oct. 17, 1849) Virtuoso Polish pianist and composer of the Romantic period, also widely regarded as one of music's most extraordinary tone poets.

Theodor Seuss Geisel (Mar. 2, 1904–Sept. 24, 1991) American bestselling children's book creator of works such as *How the Grinch Stole Christmas*, *Green Eggs and Ham*, and *The Cat In the Hat*.

Alexander Graham Bell (Mar. 3, 1847–Aug. 2, 1922) Scottish scientist, best known for his work on the telephone.

Miriam Makeba (Mar. 4, 1932– Nov. 10, 2008) South African singer who fought against apartheid in her country.

Gerardus Mercator (Mar. 5, 1512–Dec. 2, 1594) Flemish cartographer and inventor of the Mercator projection.

Michelangelo (Mar. 6, 1475– Feb. 18, 1564) Italian Renaissance painter, sculptor, architect, and poet, best known for his sculpture *David* and his painting on the Sistine Chapel's ceiling.

Maurice Ravel (Mar. 7, 1875– Dec. 28, 1937) Basque French pianist and composer of influential Impressionist music.

Cyd Charisse (Mar. 8, 1922– Jun. 17, 2008) American dancer, actress, and frequent costar of Fred Astaire and Gene Kelly.

Ornette Coleman (Mar. 9, 1930–) Innovative American saxophonist and one of the progenitors of the free jazz movement.

Harriet Tubman (ca. Mar. 10, 1820–Mar. 10, 1913) African-American abolitionist and humanitarian, responsible for guiding runaway slaves to the North before the Civil War through what is now known as the Underground Railroad.

Torquato Tasso (Mar. 11, 1544– Apr. 25, 1595) Italian Renaissance poet, best known for his epic poem "*Gerusalemme liberata* (Jerusalem Delivered)."

Jack Kerouac (Mar. 12, 1922– Oct. 21, 1969) American novelist and member of the Beat generation who was best known for his novel *On the Road*.

Al Jaffee (Mar. 13, 1921–) Satirical American cartoonist, perennial contributor to *MAD* magazine, and creator of the *MAD* fold-in, a feature on the inside back cover of the magazine.

Albert Einstein (Mar. 14, 1879– Apr. 18, 1955) German-born physicist who formulated the theory of relativity and mass-energy equivalence, $E=mc^2$.

Sam "Lightnin'" Hopkins (Mar. 15, 1912–Jan. 30, 1982) American blues guitarist known for a searing fusion of bass, rhythm lead, percussion effects, and vocals.

James Madison (Mar. 16, 1751–Jun. 28, 1836) The fourth president of the United States and principal author of the U.S. Constitution.

Mia Hamm (Mar. 17, 1972–) Former American soccer player for the United States women's national soccer team, who scored more international goals than any other player, male or female.

Queen Latifah (Mar. 18, 1970–) Popular American rapper, singer-songwriter, and actress.

Wyatt Earp (Mar. 19, 1848– Jan. 13, 1929) Iconic figure of Western American folklore.

Fred Rogers (Mar. 20, 1928– Feb. 27, 2003) American minister and host of the popular children's television show *Mister Rogers' Neighborhood*.

Johann Sebastian Bach (Mar. 21, 1685–Jul. 28, 1750) German composer whose music is considered to be the pinnacle of the Baroque tradition.

Billy Collins (Mar. 22, 1941–) Contemporary American poet and two-time U.S. Poet Laureate.

Fannie Farmer (Mar. 23, 1857– Jan. 15, 1915) American expert on cooking who edited the *Boston Cooking–School Cookbook*, a popular culinary reference tool.

William Morris (Mar. 24, 1834–Oct. 3, 1896) British artist, writer, and socialist who sought a return to medieval craftsmanship and design.

Gloria Steinem (Mar. 25, 1934–) American feminist icon, writer, and women's rights advocate.

Robert Frost (Mar. 26, 1874– Jan. 29, 1963) American poet and four-time Pulitzer Prize winner whose work was inspired by life in rural New England.

Ludwig Mies van der Rohe (Mar. 27, 1886–Aug. 17, 1969)

German-born American architect who helped introduce a new age of modern architecture.

Zbigniew Brzezinski (Mar. 28, 1928–) Polish-American political scientist who served as an advisor to President Jimmy Carter on issues of national security.

James E. Casey (Mar. 29, 1888– Jun. 6, 1983) Founder of the American Messenger Company, which is now known as the United Parcel Service.

Vincent van Gogh (Mar. 30, 1853–Jul. 29, 1890) Prodigious Dutch post-Impressionist painter whose popular works include *Starry Night* and *Sunflowers*.

César Chávez (Mar. 31, 1927– Apr. 23, 1993) Mexican-American labor leader who founded the National Farm Workers Association.

April

Wangari Maathai (Apr. 1, 1940–) The first African woman to be awarded the Nobel Peace Prize in 2004 for environmental and political activism.

Walter Percy Chrysler (Apr. 2, 1875–Aug. 18, 1940) American automobile entrepreneur and pioneer who founded the Chrysler Corporation.

Jane Goodall (Apr. 3, 1934–) British humanitarian and animal-welfare activist, widely known for her extensive primatological studies.

Maya Angelou (Apr. 4, 1928–) American modern-day Renaissance memoirist, poet, playwright, director, and civil-rights advocate who is best known for her bestselling autobiography *I Know Why the Caged Bird Sings*.

Colin Powell (Apr. 5, 1937–) Army retired general, American statesman, and the first African American appointed as United States secretary of state.

Nadar (Apr. 6, 1826–Mar. 21, 1910) French photographer credited with conducting the first photo-interview.

Billie Holiday (Apr. 7, 1915– Jul. 17, 1959) Beloved American jazz singer and author of the jazz standard "God Bless the Child."

Betty Ford (Apr. 8, 1918–) Former First Lady, founder of the Betty Ford Clinic, and recipient of a Congressional Medal.

Charles Baudelaire (Apr. 9, 1821–Aug. 31, 1867) Nineteenth-century French poet, critic, and passionate champion of Romanticism.

Rachel Corrie (Apr. 10, 1979– Mar. 16, 2003) American member

of the International Solidarity Movement, who was active in promoting peace in the Middle East and killed in Gaza during a protest mission.

Joel Grey (Apr. 11, 1932–) Award-winning American stage and screen actor, best known for his role in the Broadway musical *Cabaret*, as well as its film adaptation.

Herbie Hancock (Apr. 12, 1940–) American pianist and composer who is known for his spirited fusion of rock and soul with many forms of jazz.

Thomas Jefferson (Apr. 13, 1743– Jul. 4, 1826) Third president of the United States and author of the Declaration of Independence.

Elizabeth Huckaby (Apr. 14, 1905–Mar. 18, 1999) American educator at Little Rock Central High School, charged with protecting the five female members of the Little Rock Nine during desegregation of the school system.

Leonardo da Vinci (Apr. 15, 1452–May 2, 1519) Italian Renaissance painter, sculptor, poet, and engineer.

Wilbur Wright (Apr. 16, 1867–May 30, 1912) American aeronautical engineer who built and flew, along with his brother Orville, the world's first successful airplane.

Nikita Khrushchev (Apr. 17, 1894–Sept. 11, 1971) Soviet prime minister and first secretary of the Communist Party from 1953 to 1964.

Clarence Darrow (Apr. 18, 1857– Mar. 13, 1938) American lawyer and civil libertarian who defended John Scopes, a high school teacher accused of teaching the theory of evolution.

Merce Cunningham (Apr. 19, 1919–) American dancer and choreographer who was a soloist in the Martha Graham dance company.

Joan Miró (Apr. 20, 1893–Dec. 25, 1983) Spanish surrealist painter, ceramist, sculptor, and proponent of automatism in painting.

Charlotte Brontë (Apr. 21, 1816–Mar. 31, 1855) British Victorian novelist whose works, most notably the novel *Jane Eyre*, are among the enduring classics of English literature.

Immanuel Kant (Apr. 22, 1724– Feb. 12, 1804) Influential German philosopher of Enlightenment who was chiefly concerned with ethics, metaphysics, and epistemology.

William Shakespeare (Apr. 23, 1564–Apr. 23, 1616) Elizabethan British poet and playwright, considered the world's finest dramatist and the English language's greatest poet.

Barbra Streisand (Apr. 24, 1942–) Oscar, Emmy, Grammy, and Golden Globe Award–winning American singer, composer, political activist, and film producer and director.

Edward R. Murrow (Apr. 25, 1908–Apr. 27, 1965) Maverick American journalist made famous for his WWII broadcasts, as well as his televised attack on Joseph McCartney.

Eugène Delacroix (Apr. 26, 1798–Aug. 13, 1863) Preeminent French Romantic artist and author, most famous for his 1830 painting *Liberty Leading the People*.

Coretta Scott King (Apr. 27, 1927–Jan. 30, 2006) Wife of assassinated African-American civil-rights activist, Martin Luther King Jr., and a noted civil-rights leader, author, and singer.

Harper Lee (Apr. 28, 1926–) American novelist, best known for her Pulitzer Prize–winning novel *To Kill a Mockingbird*, for which she also received the Presidential Medal of Freedom.

Duke Ellington (Apr. 29, 1899–May 24, 1974) Virtuoso African-American composer, pianist, bandleader, notable for his contributions to jazz music.

Katherine Amelia Towle (Apr. 30, 1898–Mar. 1, 1986) American female military officer and educator who became the second director of the United States Marine Corps Women's Reserve and the first director of Women Marines.

May

Joseph Heller (May 1, 1923–Dec. 12, 1999) American writer and playwright known for his satirical WWII novel *Catch-22*.

Benjamin Spock (May 2, 1903–Mar. 15, 1998) Influential American pediatrician who authored the bestselling book *Baby and Child Care*.

Golda Meir (May 3, 1898–Dec. 8, 1978) Fourth prime minister of Israel and first woman to be elected to the position.

Audrey Hepburn (May 4, 1929–Jan. 20, 1993) Academy Award, Emmy Award, Grammy Award, and Tony Award–winning American actress, fashion icon, and UNICEF Goodwill Ambassador.

Karl Marx (May 5, 1818–Mar. 14, 1883) Nineteenth-century German philosopher, political economist, and author (with Joseph Engels) of *The Communist Manifesto* and *Das Kapital*.

Sigmund Freud (May 6, 1856–Sept. 23, 1939) Austrian psychiatrist who founded the practice of psychoanalysis and is the author of *The Interpretation of Dreams*.

Johannes Brahms (May 7, 1833–Apr. 3, 1897) German composer of the Romantic period, whose music combined elements of both the Classical and Romantic periods.

Harry S. Truman (May 8, 1884–Dec. 26, 1972) Thirty-third president of the United States and successor to Franklin D. Roosevelt, who died three months into his fourth term.

Howard Carter (May 9, 1874–Mar. 2, 1939) British archaeologist who discovered the tomb of Tutankhamun in Luxor, Egypt.

Bono (May 10, 1960–) Political activist and lead singer of the Irish rock band U2.

Martha Graham (May 11, 1894–Apr. 1, 1991) American choreographer and dancer who founded the celebrated Martha Graham Dance Company.

Florence Nightingale (May 12, 1820–Aug. 13, 1910) British nurse, hospital reformer, and founder of the Nightingale School and Home for Nurses.

Stevie Wonder (May 13, 1950–) American Grammy Award–winning singer-songwriter and record producer who signed his first record deal when he was only twelve years old.

Dante Alighieri (May 14, 1265–Sept. 14, 1321) Florentine poet and author of the epic poem *The Divine Comedy*.

L. Frank Baum (May 15, 1856–May 6, 1919) American author and creator of the popular children's book, *The Wizard of Oz*.

Louis "Studs" Terkel (May 16, 1912–Oct. 31, 2008) Pulitzer Prize–winning author and radio host who is best known for his oral histories.

Sugar Ray Leonard (May 17, 1956–) Former American professional boxer and leading boxer in the world during the late 1970s and early 1980s.

Bertrand Russell (May 18, 1872–Feb. 2, 1970) British scholar and advocate of political and social reforms, best known for his work, *Principia Mathematica*.

Malcolm X (May 19, 1925–Feb. 21, 1965) African-American Muslim human rights activist, spokesman for the Nation of Islam, and founder of the Organization of Afro-American Unity.

Jimmy Stewart (May 20, 1908–Jul. 2, 1997) Iconic American actor and recipient of the Academy Honorary Award for lifetime achievement.

Andrei Dmitrievich Sakharov (May 21, 1921–Dec. 14, 1989) Nobel Peace Prize–winning Soviet nuclear physicist and advocate of human rights and social reform in the Soviet Union.

Mary Cassatt (May 22, 1844–Jun. 14, 1926) American Impressionist painter and printmaker whose work focused on the portrayal of women.

Margaret Fuller (May 23, 1810–Jun. 19, 1850) Women's rights activist and writer of the major feminist work *Women in the Nineteenth Century*.

Bob Dylan (May 24, 1941–) Formidable American singer-songwriter, poet, musician, author, and counterculture icon of the 1960s.

Ralph Waldo Emerson (May 25, 1803–Apr. 27, 1882) American author and poet often credited with leading the Transcendentalist movement in the early nineteenth century.

Miles Davis (May 26, 1926–Sept. 28, 1991) Experimental American jazz musician and contributor to important innovations in the genre.

Julia Ward Howe (May 27, 1819–Oct. 17, 1910) American abolitionist and poet who is best known for writing "The Battle Hymn of the Republic."

Gladys Knight (May 28, 1944–) American pop and R&B singer who found success in the 1960s and 1970s under the Motown and Buddha record labels.

John F. Kennedy (May 29, 1917–Nov. 22, 1963) Thirty-fifth president of the United States who served in office from January 20, 1961 until his assassination on November 22, 1963.

Benny Goodman (May 30, 1909–Jun. 13, 1986) Prolific American jazz musician and orchestra leader.

Walt Whitman (May 31, 1819–Mar. 26, 1892) American writer who broke from traditional poetic form and created the style of free verse.

June

Morgan Freeman (Jun. 1, 1937–) Academy Award–winning American actor, film director, and film narrator.

Thomas Hardy (Jun. 2, 1840–Jan. 11, 1928) British author, poet, and exponent of the naturalist movement.

Allen Ginsberg (Jun. 3, 1926–Apr. 5, 1997) American Beat generation poet, best known for his iconoclastic poem "Howl."

Socrates (ca. Jun. 4, 470 BC–399 BC) Greek philosopher who is considered one of the founders of Western philosophy.

Bill D. Moyers (Jun. 5, 1934–) Emmy Award–winning American journalist who served as press secretary to President Lyndon B. Johnson.

Thomas Mann (Jun. 6, 1875–Aug. 12, 1955) German novelist and 1929 Nobel Prize Laureate.

Nikki Giovanni (Jun. 7, 1943–) Grammy-nominated American author, civil-rights activist, and University Distinguished Professor of English at Virginia Tech.

Frank Lloyd Wright (Jun. 8, 1867–Apr. 9, 1959) American pioneer of modern style architecture and creator of the Usonian home concept.

Michael J. Fox (Jun. 9, 1961–) Award-winning Canadian-born actor and advocate for Parkinson's Disease.

Judy Garland (Jun. 10, 1922–Jun. 22, 1969) Academy Award–winning American film actress and singer who is best known for her role as Dorothy Gale in the 1939 film *The Wizard of Oz*.

Jacques-Yves Cousteau (Jun. 11, 1910–Jun. 25, 1997) French naval officer, oceanic researcher, and documentary filmmaker.

Anne Frank (Jun. 12, 1929–Mar. 1945) German-born Jew and victim of the Holocaust, whose diary was published posthumously to worldwide acclaim.

William Butler Yeats (Jun. 13, 1865–Jan. 28, 1939) Irish poet, Nobel Prize winner, Poet Laureate, and a major figure of twentieth-century literature.

Harriet Beecher Stowe (Jun. 14, 1811–Jul. 1, 1896) American abolitionist and author who is best known for her anti-slavery novel, *Uncle Tom's Cabin*.

Saul Steinberg (Jun. 15, 1914–May 12, 1999) Romanian-born artist and cartoonist for *The New Yorker*.

Tupac Shakur (Jun. 16, 1971–Sept. 13, 1996) American hip-hop artist and social activist who was murdered in a gang-related drive-by shooting.

Igor Stravinsky (Jun. 17, 1882–Apr. 6, 1971) Influential Russian composer and conductor who is best known for his experimental and unusual form of rhythm.

Sir Paul McCartney (Jun. 18, 1942–) Grammy Award–winning British singer and songwriter who gained worldwide popularity and acclaim as one of the founding members of the Beatles.

Lou Gehrig (Jun. 19, 1903– Jun. 2, 1941) American baseball player and first baseman for the New York Yankees, who was afflicted with Amyotrophic Lateral Sclerosis, now known as Lou Gehrig's Disease.

Lillian Hellman (Jun. 20, 1905– Jun. 30, 1984) Successful American playwright and the first woman to have been nominated for an Academy Award for original screenplay.

Jean-Paul Sartre (Jun. 21, 1905– Apr. 15, 1980) French philosopher, dramatist, writer, and promoter of existentialism.

Erich Maria Remarque (Jun. 22, 1898–Sept. 25, 1970) German author most famous for his autobiographical WWI novel *All Quiet on the Western Front.*

Anna Gorenko (Jun. 23, 1889– Mar. 5, 1966) Russian poet and leader of the St. Petersburg Acmeist movement.

Robert Reich (Jun. 24, 1946–) American politician and twenty-second secretary of labor of the United States who served under President Bill Clinton.

George Orwell (Jun. 25, 1903– Jan. 21, 1950) British political essayist, satirist, and author of the antitotalitarian novels *1984* and *Animal Farm.*

Derek Jeter (Jun. 26, 1974–) American Major League Baseball player, nine-time all-star shortstop, and current captain of the New York Yankees.

Helen Keller (Jun. 27, 1880– Jun. 1, 1968) American deaf and blind activist who overcame her disabilities to become the first deaf-blind person to graduate from college.

Mel Brooks (Jun. 28, 1926–) Multiple award-winning American director, writer, producer, and entertainer, best known for his comedic films and slapstick humor.

Antoine de Saint-Exupéry (Jun. 29, 1900–Jul. 31, 1944) French writer, aviator, and author of the novella *The Little Prince.*

Robert D. Ballard (Jun. 30, 1942–) Oceanographer and underwater archaeologist, best known for his discovery of the wreck of the RMS *Titanic.*

July

Lady Diana Spencer (Jul. 1, 1961– Aug. 31, 1997) Public figure and first wife of Charles, Prince of Wales, who died tragically in an automobile accident.

Hermann Hesse (Jul. 2, 1877– Aug. 9, 1962) German-Swiss poet, painter, and recipient of the Nobel Prize for literature.

Franz Kafka (Jul. 3, 1883–Jun. 3, 1924) German fiction author, best known for the short story "The Metamorphosis" and the novels *The Trial* and *The Castle.*

Nathaniel Hawthorne (Jul. 4, 1804–May 19, 1864) American author, best known for his tales of America's colonial history and his book *The Scarlet Letter.*

Chuck Close (Jul. 5, 1940–) American photo-realist painter of larger-than-life portraits who was left severely paralyzed because of a spinal artery collapse.

Frida Kahlo (Jul. 6, 1907–Jul. 13, 1954) Mexican painter and wife of artist Diego Rivero, best known for her highly symbolic self-portraits that draw on Mexican culture and on European traditions.

Satchel Paige (Jul. 7, 1905– Jun. 8, 1982) Legendary Baseball Hall of Fame inductee and first African-American athlete to play Major League Baseball.

Elisabeth Kübler-Ross (Jul. 8, 1926–Aug. 24, 2004) Psychiatrist who outlined the five stages of grief in what is known as the Elisabeth Kübler-Ross Grief Cycle.

Tom Hanks (Jul. 9, 1956–) Popular Academy Award–winning American actor, director, writer, and producer who is known for his successful roles in films such as *Forrest Gump, Philadelphia,* and *Apollo 13.*

Arthur Ashe (Jul. 10, 1943– Feb. 6, 1993) Prominent African-American tennis player and winner of three Grand Slam titles.

E. B. White (Jul. 11, 1899– Oct. 1, 1985) American writer of the celebrated children's book *Charlotte's Web.*

Henry David Thoreau (Jul. 12, 1817–May 6, 1862) American Transcendentalist writer and naturalist whose book *Walden* remains his most popular work.

Erno Rubik (Jul. 13, 1944–) Hungarian inventor of the mathematical puzzle known as the Rubik's Cube.

Woody Guthrie (Jul. 14, 1912– Oct. 3, 1967) Socially conscious Depression-era American songwriter, folk musician, and composer of the song "This Land Is Your Land."

Thomas Bulfinch (Jul. 15, 1796– May 27, 1867) American writer and author of *Bulfinch's Mythology,* a compilation of his works.

Ida B. Wells-Barnett (Jul. 16, 1862–Mar. 25, 1931) African-American journalist, civil-rights and women's rights advocate, and an active participant in the women's suffrage movement.

Berenice Abbott (Jul. 17, 1898– Dec. 9, 1991) American photographer whose style commonly consisted of black-and-white photographs of New York City and other urban areas.

Nelson Mandela (Jul. 18, 1918–) Anti-apartheid activist, Nobel Peace Prize Laureate, and the first president of South Africa to be democratically elected.

Edgar Degas (Jul. 19, 1834– Sept. 27, 1917) Masterful French painter, printmaker, sculptor, draftsman, and early exponent of Impressionism.

Sir Edmund Hillary (Jul. 20, 1919–Jan. 11, 2008) New Zealand explorer, mountain climber, and one of the first people to reach the summit of Mt. Everest.

Ernest Hemingway (Jul. 21, 1899– Jul. 2, 1961) American author of the Pulitzer Prize–winning novel *The Old Man and the Sea.*

Edward Hopper (Jul. 22, 1882– May 15, 1967) Modern American realist painter, printmaker, and creator of iconic images celebrating urban and rural America.

Raymond Chandler (Jul. 23, 1888–Mar. 26, 1959) Author who greatly influenced the modern depiction of a private detective through his fictional crime stories and novels.

Amelia Earhart (Jul. 24, 1897- Jan. 5, 1939) American aviator and recipient of the Distinguished Flying Cross as the first woman to fly solo across the Atlantic Ocean.

Thomas Eakins (Jul. 25, 1844– Jun. 25, 1916) Preeminent American realist painter who is known for introducing the experience of American life in his work rather than adhering to European traditions.

Aldous Huxley (Jul. 26, 1894– Nov. 22, 1963) British writer and author of the famous science-fiction novel *Brave New World.*

Norman Lear (Jul. 27, 1922–) American television writer and producer of numerous popular television sitcoms, such as *All in the Family* and *The Jeffersons.*

Jacqueline Kennedy Onassis (Jul. 28, 1929–May 19, 1994) Former wife of John F. Kennedy and First Lady of the United States until her husband's assassination on November 22, 1963.

Alexis de Tocqueville (Jul. 29, 1805–Apr. 16, 1859) French political philosopher and author of *Democracy in America.*

Henry Ford (Jul. 30, 1863– Apr. 7, 1947) American founder of the Ford Motor Company and the inventor of the modern assembly line.

J. K. Rowling (Jul. 31, 1965–) British writer and author of the bestselling Harry Potter fantasy series.

August

Yves Saint Laurent (Aug. 1, 1936–) French fashion designer whose style combines casual with couture.

James A. Baldwin (Aug. 2, 1924– Nov. 30, 1987) African-American writer and playwright, known for exploring sociological issues, such as race and orientation, through his works.

Martha Stewart (Aug. 3, 1941–) American businesswoman who created a successful empire based on homemaking and lifestyle technique.

Barack Obama (Aug. 4, 1961–) Democrat and first African-American to be elected the forty-fourth president of the United States.

Neil Armstrong (Aug. 5, 1930–) American astronaut who is the first person to have set foot on the moon.

Andy Warhol (Aug. 6, 1928– Feb. 22, 1987) American artist and a central figure in the Pop Art movement.

Garrison Keillor (Aug. 7, 1942–) American writer and radio personality, best known as the host of the Minnesota Public Radio show "A Prairie Home Companion."

Emiliano Zapata (Aug. 8, 1879– Apr. 10, 1919) Central figure in the Mexican Revolution and commander of the Liberation Army.

Marvin Minsky (Aug. 9, 1927–) American scientist and cofounder of MIT's artificial intelligence laboratory.

Herbert Hoover (Aug. 10, 1874– Oct. 20, 1964) Thirty-first president of the United States during the beginning of the Great Depression.

Alex Haley (Aug. 11, 1921– Feb. 10, 1992) African-American author of *Roots: The Saga of an American Family* and *The Autobiography of Malcolm X.*

Cecil B. DeMille (Aug. 12, 1881– Jan. 22, 1959) Academy Award–winning filmmaker whose movies were grand and extravagant in style.

Sir Alfred Hitchcock (Aug. 13, 1899–Apr. 29, 1980) Highly influential British film producer and director of critically acclaimed suspense and thriller movies, such as *Psycho* and *Vertigo*.

Steve Martin (Aug. 14, 1945–) Emmy and Grammy Award–winning American actor and comedian.

Julia Child (Aug. 15, 1912–Aug. 13, 2004) American cook, author, and television personality who specialized in French cuisine.

Madonna (Aug. 16, 1958–) Successful American pop singer and entertainer, known for her controversial image throughout her career.

Davy Crockett (Aug. 17, 1786–Mar. 6, 1836) American folk hero and frontiersman who died defending the Alamo in 1836.

Robert Redford (Aug. 18, 1936–) Academy Award–winning movie director and actor who founded the Sundance Film Festival.

William Jefferson Clinton (Aug. 19, 1946–) Forty-second president of the United States and first Democrat since FDR to win a second term.

Robert Plant (August 20, 1948–) British lead vocalist and songwriter for the rock band Led Zeppelin, and winner of five Grammy Awards.

William "Count" Basie (Aug. 21, 1904–Apr. 26, 1984) African-American jazz pianist, composer, and leader of the Count Basie Orchestra.

Claude Debussy (Aug. 22, 1862–Mar. 25, 1918) French Impressionist composer and an influential figure in the symbolism movement.

Edgar Lee Masters (Aug. 23, 1869–Mar. 5, 1950) American biographer who authored a collection of poems titled *The Spoon River Anthology*.

Jorge Luis Borges (Aug. 24, 1899–Jun. 14, 1986) Bilingual Argentine writer, poet, and translator.

Althea Gibson (Aug. 25, 1927–Sept. 28, 2003) American tennis player who, in 1956, became the first African-American woman to win a Grand Slam title.

Blessed Mother Teresa (Aug. 26, 1910–Sept. 5, 1997) Revered Roman Catholic nun and founder of the Missionaries of Charity in Calcutta, India.

Georg Wilhelm Friedrich Hegel (Aug. 27, 1770–Nov. 14, 1831) German philosopher and one of the chief exponents of German idealism.

Rita Dove (Aug. 28, 1952–) First African-American woman to be honored as the youngest Poet Laureate of the United States.

Charlie Parker (Aug. 29, 1920–Mar. 12, 1955) American jazz musician and a driving force in the development of bebop.

Robert Crumb (Aug. 30, 1943–) American artist and a founder of the underground comics movement.

Van Morrison (Aug. 31, 1945–) Grammy Award–winning Irish rock singer, and songwriter.

September

Lily Tomlin (Sept. 1, 1939–) Emmy and Tony Award–winning actress and comedienne.

Christa McAuliffe (Sept. 2, 1948–Jan. 28, 1986) American teacher selected to participate in the NASA Teacher in Space Project, whose life ended aboard the space shuttle *Challenger*.

Louis Sullivan (Sept. 3, 1856–Apr. 14, 1924) Modernist American architect considered by many to have invented the modern skyscraper.

Richard Wright (Sept. 4, 1908–Nov. 28, 1960) African-American author concerned with race relations and the African-American experience.

Louis XIV (Sept. 5, 1638–Sept. 1, 1715) The "Sun King" of France and Navarre, believed to be the longest reigning monarch (seventy-two years) in European history.

Jane Addams (Sept. 6, 1860–May 21, 1935) A pioneer of social work and feminism who founded the Settlement House Movement in 1931, and was the first American female recipient of the Nobel Peace Prize.

Grandma Moses (Sept. 7, 1860–Dec. 13, 1961) American folk artist, best known for starting her artistic career at the age of seventy-six.

Patsy Cline (Sept. 8, 1932–Mar. 5, 1963) Acclaimed American country music star who is best known for her rendition of Willie Nelson's song, "Crazy."

Cesare Pavese (Sept. 9, 1908–Aug. 27, 1950) Renowned Italian poet and novelist who is notable for his theme of the isolated loner betrayed by society.

Roger Maris (Sept. 10, 1934–Dec. 14, 1985) American Major League Baseball player who famously broke the single-season home-run record that was previously held by Babe Ruth.

O. Henry (Sept. 11, 1862–Jun. 5, 1910) American writer of more than four hundred short stories that are known for their sharp wit, brilliant wordplay, and use of surprise endings.

Jesse Owens (Sept. 12, 1913–Mar. 31, 1980) African-American track-and-field athlete and winner of four gold medals at the 1936 Olympics in Berlin, Germany.

Roald Dahl (Sept. 13, 1916–Nov. 23, 1990) Bestselling Welsh children's novelist, short-story author, and screenwriter who is best known for his works *Charlie and the Chocolate Factory*, *James and the Giant Peach*, and *Matilda*.

Allan Bloom (Sept. 14, 1930–Oct. 7, 1992) American philosopher, literary critic, and core proponent of the Great Books academic program.

Dame Agatha Christie (Sept. 15, 1890–Jan. 12, 1976) British crime fiction writer who created the characters Hercule Poirot and Miss Marple, and was one of the bestselling authors of all time.

B. B. King (Sept. 16, 1925–) African-American blues guitarist and singer who was named the third-best guitarist of all time by *Rolling Stone* magazine.

Hank Williams (Sept. 17, 1923–Jan. 1, 1953) Prolific American singer and songwriter who was the chief proponent of the honky-tonk style, as well as being a country music icon.

Lance Armstrong (Sept. 18, 1971–) American professional cyclist who, after a life-threatening bout with cancer, was the winner of seven consecutive Tours de France.

Sir William Golding (Sept. 19, 1911–Jun. 19, 1993) British author, Nobel Prize Laureate, and Booker Prize recipient; most famously known for his novel, *Lord of the Flies*.

Sophia Loren (Sept. 20, 1934–) Italian Academy Award–winning actress, sex symbol, singer, and wife of movie producer Carlo Ponti.

Stephen King (Sept. 21, 1947–) American author of more than two hundred books, including more than fifty bestselling horror and fantasy novels.

Andrea Bocelli (Sept. 22, 1958–) Popular blind Italian singer who has a proven crossover success between operatic and pop songs.

Ray Charles (Sept. 23, 1930–Jun. 10, 2004) Famous blind African-American rhythm-and-blues pianist/singer who is best known for songs like "Georgia On My Mind" and "Hit the Road, Jack."

Linda McCartney (Sept. 24, 1941–Apr. 17, 1998) American photographer, vegan cookbook author, animal-rights' activist, and late wife of the Beatles' singer, Sir Paul McCartney.

William Faulkner (Sept. 25, 1897–Jul. 6, 1962) Influential Nobel Prize–winning American novelist and poet who is noted for his experimental "stream of consciousness" writing style.

Ivan Pavlov (Sept. 26, 1849–Feb. 27, 1936) Nobel Prize–winning Russian researcher, psychologist, and physiologist who is famous for his discovery of and experiments with the "conditioned reflex."

Samuel Adams (Sept. 27, 1722–Oct. 2, 1803) American Founding Father, political philosopher, and, politician.

Ed Sullivan (Sept. 28, 1901–Oct. 13, 1974) American television star, famously known as the emcee of his eponymous TV variety show, *The Ed Sullivan Show*.

Michelangelo Antonioni (Sept. 29, 1912–Jul. 30, 2007) Italian film director whose minimalist style had a tremendous influence on post-neorealist Italian film.

Truman Capote (Sept. 30, 1924–Aug. 25, 1984) Internationally acclaimed American writer, best known for the nonfiction novel *In Cold Blood* and the novella *Breakfast at Tiffany's*.

October

Jimmy Carter (Oct. 1, 1924–) Thirty-ninth president of the United States and recipient of the Nobel Peace Prize in 2002 for his work promoting global health, democracy, and human rights.

Mahatma Gandhi (Oct. 2, 1869–Jan. 30, 1948) Influential Indian leader of the Indian independence movement, famous for his peaceful call for civil disobedience and nonviolence.

Gore Vidal (Oct. 3, 1925–) American author of novels, plays, screenplays, and essays, as well as an outspoken critic of the American political establishment.

Buster Keaton (Oct. 4, 1895–Feb. 1, 1966) American silent-film comic actor and Academy Award filmmaker whose films were famous for their athletic comedy.

Václav Havel (Oct. 5, 1936–) Czech writer, poet, and dramatist who was not only the last president of Czechoslovakia but also the first president of the newly formed Czech Republic.

Fannie Lou Hamer (Oct. 6, 1917–Mar. 14, 1977) African-American civil-rights champion and activist, especially in the field of voter equality.

Desmond Tutu (Oct. 7, 1931–) Nobel Peace Prize–winning South African activist who fought for equal human rights, and fought against apartheid.

Jesse Jackson (Oct. 8, 1941–) African-American civil-rights leader and minister, and founder of the Rainbow/PUSH organization, which fights for equality and antidiscrimination.

John Lennon (Oct. 9, 1940– Dec. 8, 1980) British songwriter, singer, peace activist, and one of the founding members of the Beatles who was tragically murdered at the age of forty.

Thelonious Monk (Oct. 10, 1917– Feb. 17, 1982) Improvisational jazz pianist and musician who is widely thought to have founded bebop.

Eleanor Roosevelt (Oct. 11, 1884–Nov. 7, 1962) American First Lady and wife to President Franklin D. Roosevelt. She used her influence to support her husband's New Deal policies.

Luciano Pavarotti (Oct. 12, 1935– Sept. 6, 2007) Italian tenor who dabbled in pop music and was known as one of the most beloved performers of all time.

Margaret Thatcher (Oct. 13, 1925–) The first female British prime minister and the first woman to lead the Conservative Party.

e. e. cummings (Oct. 14, 1894– Sept. 3, 1962), American avant-garde poet, artist, and writer, best remembered for his unusual and unconventional use of grammar and syntax.

Isabella Bird (Oct. 15, 1831– Oct. 7, 1904) British adventuress, nineteenth-century world traveler, writer, and the first woman inducted into the National Geographic Society.

Oscar Wilde (Oct. 16, 1854– Nov. 30, 1900) Late Victorian Irish playwright, novelist, and poet, known for his flamboyance.

Evel Knievel (Oct. 17, 1938– Nov. 30, 2007) Seemingly fearless American motorcycle daredevil and entertainer who was made famous for his broadcasted motorcycle jumps.

Chuck Berry (Oct. 18, 1926–) Iconic African-American pioneer of rock and roll, and composer of such classics as "Roll Over Beethoven" and "Johnny B. Goode."

John le Carré (Oct. 19, 1931–) British novelist of spy-thriller novels revolving around the Cold War, the most celebrated being *The Spy Who Came in From the Cold.*

Mickey Mantle (Oct. 20, 1931– Aug. 13, 1995) National Baseball Hall of Fame inductee, and famous New York Yankees ballplayer who continues to hold several major league records.

Alfred Nobel (Oct. 21 1833– Dec. 10, 1896) Swedish chemist and engineer who is considered to be the inventor of dynamite and the founder of the Nobel Prize.

Doris Lessing (Oct. 22, 1919–) Nobel Prize–winning British writer, anti-apartheid activist, and author of *The Golden Notebook.*

Pelé (Oct. 23, 1940–) Former Brazilian soccer star, Athlete of the Century, and member of the National Soccer Hall of Fame.

Paula Gunn Allen (Oct. 24, 1939–) Native American poet, anthropological writer, and novelist who is famous for her studies of Native American female life.

Pablo Picasso (Oct. 25, 1881– Apr. 8, 1973) Spanish founder of the Cubist school of painting, most famously known for pieces such as *Les Demoiselles d'Avignon* and *Guernica.*

Hillary Rodham Clinton (Oct. 26, 1947–) Former First Lady to President Bill Clinton, the first First Lady elected into the Senate, and secretary of state serving under President Barack Obama.

Dylan Thomas (Oct. 27, 1914– Nov. 9, 1953) Welsh modernist poet and author, recognized notably for "Do Not Go Gentle Into That Good Night" and *Under Milk Wood.*

Jonas Edward Salk (Oct. 28, 1914–Jun. 23, 1995) American biologist and physician, renowned for uncovering the first effective polio vaccine, known as the Salk vaccine.

James Boswell (Oct. 29, 1740– May 19, 1795) Author of Samuel Johnson's biography and whose surname has become an English term for "a person who records in detail the life of a usually famous contemporary."

Ezra Pound (Oct. 30, 1885– Nov. 1, 1972) American expatriate poet and Modernist who was a major figure of early to mid-twentieth-century poetry.

John Keats (Oct. 31, 1795– Feb. 23, 1821) British Romantic poet, known as a preeminent member of the movement and most recognized for his odes.

November

Stephen Crane (Nov. 1, 1871– Jun. 5, 1900) American realist and naturalist author whose most well-known work is *The Red Badge of Courage.*

Marie-Antoinette (Nov. 2, 1755– Oct. 16, 1793) Austrian queen of France and wife to King Louis XVI and was beheaded during the French Revolution.

Benvenuto Cellini (Nov. 3, 1500– Feb. 13, 1571) Italian Renaissance man whose various occupations spanned from military man to musician, painter to autobiographer.

Walter Cronkite (Nov. 4, 1916–) Retired American broadcast journalist and anchor for *The CBS Evening News,* commonly referred to as "the most trusted man in America."

Sam Shepard (Nov. 5, 1943–) American award–winning playwright, Academy Award–nominated author, and stage and film director.

John Philip Sousa (Nov. 6, 1854– Mar. 8, 1932) American composer who is dubbed "the March King" and is recognized mainly for his military-style marches and compositions.

Albert Camus (Nov. 7, 1913– Jan. 4, 1960) Nobel Prize–winning French Existentialist author and philosopher whose most famous novel is *The Plague.*

Edmond Halley (Nov. 8, 1656– Jan. 14, 1742) British scientist and mathematician who specialized in astronomy and meteorology and discovered a comet now known as Halley's comet.

Anne Sexton (Nov. 9, 1928– Oct. 4, 1974) American confessional poet and writer who is famous for poems such as "The Double Image."

Martin Luther (Nov. 10, 1483– Feb. 18, 1546) German monk and theological reformer who founded Protestantism after confronting the worldly corruption of the Roman Catholic Church during the Middle Ages.

Kurt Vonnegut Jr. (Nov. 11, 1922–Apr. 11, 2007) American novelist, known for blending dark comedy, satiric elements, and science fiction, and whose books include *Slaughterhouse-Five* and *Cat's Cradle.*

Grace Kelly (Nov. 12, 1929– Sept. 14, 1982) Academy Award–winning American actress who not only became the princess of Monaco but who also ranks as one of the AFI's Greatest Female Stars of All Time.

Robert Louis Stevenson (Nov. 13, 1850–Dec. 3, 1894) Scottish neo-Romantic writer who is best known for his novels *Treasure Island* and *The Strange Case of Dr. Jekyll and Mr. Hyde.*

Claude Monet (Nov. 14, 1840– Dec. 5, 1926) Leading exponent of French Impressionist painting whose most famous works include *Bridge Over a Pond of Water Lilies* and *Water Lilies.*

Georgia O'Keeffe (Nov. 15, 1887– Mar. 6, 1986) Modern American painter, member of the American Academy of Arts and Letters, and purveyor of the American southwest who is most recognized for her abstracted images of flowers.

W. C. Handy (Nov. 16, 1873– Mar. 28, 1958) African-American "Father of the Blues," jazz composer, musician, and author.

Martin Scorsese (Nov. 17, 1942–) Italian-American Academy Award–winning director, producer, and writer who directed the classic films *Raging Bull, Taxi Driver,* and *Goodfellas.*

George Horace Gallup (Nov. 18, 1901–Jul. 26, 1984) American statistician who invented a poll, later called the Gallup poll, which gauged public opinion via the use of surveys.

Ted Turner (Nov. 19, 1938–) American media mogul and philanthropist who founded the first twenty-four-hour cable news channel, CNN.

Robert F. Kennedy (Nov. 20, 1925–Jun. 6, 1968) United States attorney general and New York senator who was the martyred sibling of U.S. President John F. Kennedy.

René Magritte (Nov. 21, 1898– Aug. 15, 1967) Belgian surrealist painter and creator of witty and satirical works, most famous for his piece *The Treachery of Images.*

Billie Jean King (Nov. 22, 1943–) Retired American female tennis player and founder of the Women's Tennis Association, who held several records in both singles and doubles tennis.

Boris Karloff (Nov. 23, 1887– Feb. 2, 1969) British stage and film actor who is best known for his portrayal of Frankenstein's monster in the 1931 film *Frankenstein.*

Henri de Toulouse-Lautrec (Nov. 24, 1864–Sept. 9, 1901) Post-Impressionist French painter who specialized in portraying the seedy underbelly of Paris nightlife.

Joe DiMaggio (Nov. 25, 1914– Mar. 8, 1999) National Baseball Hall of Fame inductee and center fielder for the New York Yankees.

Sojourner Truth (ca. Nov. 26, 1797–Nov. 26, 1883) Former African-American slave, abolitionist, and activist for women's rights.

Jimi Hendrix (Nov. 27, 1942– Sept. 18, 1970) American rock guitarist and performer whose considerable virtuosity on the instrument made him a legend.

William Blake (Nov. 28, 1757–Aug. 12, 1827) British Romantic poet and painter who is most recognized for his two poetry compilations, *Song of Innocence* and *Songs of Experience*.

Louisa May Alcott (Nov. 29, 1832–Mar. 6, 1888) American novelist who is most famous for her 1868 novel, *Little Women*.

Sir Winston Churchill (Nov. 30, 1874–Jan. 24,1965) Two-time British prime minister and Nobel Prize Laureate who is most recognized for his leadership during WWII.

December

Woody Allen (Dec. 1, 1935–) Three-time Academy Award–winning American film director, comedian, screenwriter, and actor who is best known for his nervous comedy, which was featured in movies like *Annie Hall*.

Maria Callas (Dec. 2, 1923–Sept. 16, 1977) American operatic soprano who is known for her extremely adaptable voice.

Jean-Luc Godard (Dec. 3, 1930–) French New Wave filmmaker whose films are famous for questioning and deconstructing classical Hollywood narrative and technique.

Rainer Maria Rilke (Dec. 4 1875–Dec. 29, 1926) Twentieth-century German poet who is often considered the bridge between traditional and modern poetry.

Walt Disney (Dec. 5, 1901–Dec. 15, 1966) Record-holding Academy Award–winning animator who created one of the most recognizable cartoon characters in the history of the world, Mickey Mouse.

Ira Gershwin (Dec. 6, 1896–Aug. 17, 1983) American lyricist of some of the most famous songs and Broadway musicals of the past century, chiefly among them "Summertime" and "Someone to Watch Over Me."

Willa Cather (Dec. 7, 1873–Apr. 24, 1947) Nebraskan author and chronicler of Great Plains frontier life, whose works include *My Antonia* and *O Pioneers!*

James Thurber (Dec. 8, 1894–Nov. 2, 1961) American writer and cartoonist who is famous for the humorous sketches and short stories he contributed to *The New Yorker* magazine.

John Milton (Dec. 9, 1608–Nov. 8, 1674) British writer, civil servant for the English Commonwealth, and liberalist who is renowned for the epic poem *Paradise Lost*.

Emily Dickinson (Dec. 10, 1830–May 15, 1886) Nineteenth-century American poet and recluse whose most prolific work wasn't published until after her death.

John Kerry (Dec. 11, 1943–) Junior United States Massachusetts senator and chairman of the Foreign Relations Committee, who was a 2004 nominee for the Democratic Party.

William Lloyd Garrison (Dec. 12, 1805–May 24, 1879) Prominent American abolitionist, journalist, and social reformer.

Dick Van Dyke (Dec. 13, 1925–) Emmy, Tony, and Grammy Award–winning American actor, comedian, and dancer who is best known for his role in *Mary Poppins*.

Shirley Jackson (Dec. 14, 1919–Aug. 8, 1965) American author who is best known for her short story "The Lottery" and her horror novel *The Haunting of Hill House*.

Julie Taymor (Dec. 15, 1952–) American Broadway and film director, notable as the first female musical director to win a Tony Award and as the creator of *The Lion King*.

Margaret Mead (Dec. 16, 1901–Nov. 15, 1978) American cultural anthropologist and author of *Coming of Age in Samoa*, whose work had a great impact on the culture of the 1960s in America.

Ludwig van Beethoven (Dec. 17, 1770–Mar. 26, 1827) Deaf German composer, virtuoso pianist, and pivotal figure in the transition from eighteenth-century musical Classicism to nineteenth-century Romanticism, whose great works include "Für Elise" and his fifth and ninth symphonies.

Steven Spielberg (Dec. 18, 1946–) Academy Award–winning American director, producer, and the highest grossing filmmaker of all time, famous for cinema classics like *E.T.: The Extra-Terrestrial*, *Schindler's List*, and *Jaws*.

Édith Piaf (Dec. 19, 1915–Oct. 11, 1963) Popular French singer and national icon, whose most famous piece is the ballad "La Vie En Rose."

Jean Racine (Dec. 20, 1639–Apr. 21, 1699) Preeminent seventeenth-century French dramatist, tragedian, and poet.

Frank Zappa (Dec. 21, 1940–Dec. 4, 1993) Iconoclastic American pop musician, composer, film director, and freedom of speech advocate who was awarded the 1997 Grammy Lifetime Achievement Award.

Giacomo Puccini (Dec. 22, 1858–Nov. 29, 1924) Immensely popular Italian composer of operas, sacred music, and chamber music, whose most famous works include *La Bohème* and *Madama Butterfly*.

Sarah Breedlove Walker (Dec. 23, 1867–May 25, 1919) African-American businesswoman and designer of hair-care products specifically made for black women.

Joseph Cornell (Dec. 24, 1903–Dec. 29, 1972) American avant-garde sculptor and filmmaker, as well as a pioneer of the assemblage idea of three-dimensional design.

Clara Barton (Dec. 25, 1821–Apr. 12, 1912) American nurse, humanitarian, suffragist, and abolitionist who organized the American Red Cross.

Henry Miller (Dec. 26, 1891–Jun. 7, 1980) American author, literary critic, and artist whose most recognized work is the 1934 novel *Tropic of Cancer*.

Marlene Dietrich (Dec. 27, 1901–May 6, 1992) German-born actress and singer, whose filmography includes *The Blue Angel* and *Shanghai Express*, and whose most famous recording was "Falling In Love Again (Can't Help It)."

Woodrow Wilson (Dec. 28, 1856–Feb. 3, 1924) Twenty-eighth Democratic president of the United States whose progressive politics included antitrust laws, the Federal Trade Commission, and the Federal Reserve Act.

Mary Tyler Moore (Dec. 29, 1936–) Award-winning American comedic actress who is best known for her television roles, most notably as Mary in the eponymous *Mary Tyler Moore Show*.

Tiger Woods (Dec. 30, 1975–) American professional golf player, former child prodigy, and one of the highest-ranked golfers and highest-paid athletes.

Odetta Holmes (Dec. 31, 1930–Dec. 2, 2008) Legendary African-American blues and jazz singer, guitarist, and preeminent figure in the 1950s and 1960s popularity of American folk music.

Index

Page numbers in roman indicate where you can find that person's quote. Page numbers in italic indicate where you can find that person's bio.